Mapped In or Mapped Out?

The Romanian Poor in Inter-household and Community Networks

Maria Amelina
Dan Chiribuca
Stephen Knack

THE WORLD BANK
Washington, D.C.

ISBN: 0-8213-5888-X
eISBN: 0-8213-5889-8
ISSN: 1726-5878

Maria Amelina is Senior Social Development Specialist in the Environmentally and Socially Sustainable Development unit of the Europe and Central Asia Region at the World Bank. Dan Chiribuca is Associate Professor of Sociology and Social Work at "Babes-Bolyai" University and Research Director at the Metro Media Transilvania Institute of Social Studies, Polls, Marketing and Advertising in Cluj-Napoca, Romania.

Library of Congress Cataloging-in-Publication Data has been requested.

TABLE OF CONTENTS

ACKNOWLEDGMENTS

Many colleagues contributed to the design, data collection, and analysis. We thank Emanuela Galasso, Philip Keefer, Ghazala Mansuri, Alexandre Marc, Dena Ringold, and Claire Wallace for helpful and insightful comments. Alina Barsan assisted in the design of the survey and in the data collection. Nils Junge and Victor Giosan provided background information. Mirca Comsa, Lu Wang, and Min Ouyang assisted in data analyses. Leah Cohen and Diana Marginean edited and formatted the final version. We also would like to thank the public officials, NGO leaders, and experts who participated in seminars held in Bukharest, Cluj, and Iasi for feedback and suggestions.

The Institute of Advanced Studies (IHS) and Metro Media Transilvania helped to design the study and carry out the field work. The World Bank Resident Mission in Romania, most prominently Richard Florescu, helped with the logistics. Indicators on Local Democratic Governance in CEE designed by the Tocqueville Research Center and the Local Government and Public Service Reform Initiative (LGI) of the Open Society Institute (Hungary) informed the design of the public officials' questionnaire used in the survey.

We gratefully acknowledge the grant from the Austrian Trust Fund.

All errors and omissions are ours.

CHAPTER 1

INTRODUCTION

S adly, all societies have a sizeable share of economically disadvantaged. Does this economic disadvantage translate into a social one? How do the two interact? At different stages of economic development and collective consciousness, both individual social groups as well as countries search for answers to the former, while social scientists seek to provide different explanations for the latter. In modern richer economies the accepted practice is for the state to formally redistribute resources in the form of public transfers to more vulnerable groups. The danger of such a formalized arrangement in the eyes of some prominent economists (Becker 1974, Barro 1974) has been the "crowding out" of private informal transfers—a traditional form of support among households. Empirically, however, no consistent evidence of such a "crowd out" effect has been found. At the formal societal level, the phenomenon is explained by a long tradition of public support in developed countries as well as by a long and growing tradition of private philanthropic giving (Cox etal. 1999). At the informal household level, even though time series for private transfers of equal length are lacking, there has been no evidence of the replacement of private transfers by public flows (Cox and Jakubson 1995, King and McDonald 1999, Ward-Batts 2001). Regardless of interpretations for such transfers, be it altruistic giving (Andreoni 1989, Samuelson 1993, Coate 1995, Barrett 1999) or an insurance mechanism (Coate and Ravallion 1993, Platteau 1995), informal transfers are observed to flow to poorer relatives.

In the developing countries, due to the paucity of formal public flows, the pro-poor nature of informal transactions stands out yet more dramatically as inter-household transfers are observed to play the role of means-tested benefits. (Gibson etal. 1998, Cox etal. 1999, Cox 2002, Jimenez etal. 2001).

Where does this leave the transition economies? On the one hand, post-socialist states have a tradition of non-targeted universal state support, arguably, creating a culture of dependency (Milanovic 1995). On the other hand, the need to obtain goods informally in a shortage economy in conjunction with the oppressive nature of the state and the desire of a large share of the population to hide from its controlling eye, breed mistrust of collective action in general and of the community members with whom they are not personally familiar in particular (Verdery 1996, Ledeneva 1998, Scott 1998).

How do these dynamics reflect on the position of the poor in society and in social and economic networks? In post-socialist times in Central European countries in general and in Romania in particular strong social ties connecting relatives, immediate friends and associates are observed to have become stronger, while the weak ties connecting individuals and households through professional and social associations have become weaker (Manning etal. 2000, Toth and Sik 2002, Stanculescu 2002). The poor are reported to be falling out of both types of associations. Strong familial and friendly networks have become difficult to maintain because of high maintenance costs, such as reciprocal gift giving and costs of transportation and telecommunication. Weak associational networks have become less accessible to the poor as well, due to the high costs of accessing newly reconfigured social networks on the one hand and the disassociation from old networks through loss of employment and migration to rural areas on the other. Another reported reason for the low levels of inclusion of the poor in voluntary organizations in the post-communist states may be the *de facto* closed, elitist nature of formal associational life. These patterns of voluntary mobilization contrast with the bridging role of associations in western democracies and need to be examined in greater detail (Uslaner 2003). It is also important to assess more precisely if these conflicting trends lead to a double exclusion of the poor from private and public, formal and informal networks. Such exclusion is likely to lead to increased vulnerability, inability to adjust to the realities of the market environment, and, therefore, increased dependency on the state for immediate subsistence and for reintegration into broader social networks and the labor force. Better understanding of the whole universe of exchanges accessible or not accessible to poor households is very important to make public policies of redistribution more sensitive to these trends and thus better targeted.

Description of the Study

This volume analyses patterns of economic and social interactions that sustain the poor or, alternatively, isolate them yet further from other households, from the communities in which they live and, by extension, from social networks and economic opportunities. The study also assesses interactions of the poor with local and central government in terms of the level of trust and satisfaction with public officials, the level of involvement in public actions and public decision-making, and the ability of local governments to respond to the needs of their poorer constituency, especially in providing social assistance and other Minimum Income Guarantee (MIG) benefits.

This study examines the associations that have not been adequately considered when assessing the well-being of the poor. These are:

- transfers between poor households and formal private associations;
- transfers made to and from poor households within informal inter-household networks—(friends, relatives, close associates);
- association between the level of income of a household and a community, and participation in collective action and local government decision-making;
- effects of legacy (historical forms of governance) and ethnicity on patterns of trust in local government, public interaction, and perceived corruption.

Mapping out the universe of these interactions from the position of the poor is the primary goal of this analysis.

To study patterns of formal and informal transfers and relate them to the characteristics of households and of communities, a nationally representative household survey was carried out. The survey covers household income and transactions for 2002 and includes expanded sections on: 1) informal inter-household transactions (gift giving, exchanges, and barter), 2) channels through which resources flow to and from households (between relatives, friends, and other informal associates), and 3) forms these flows take (cash, goods, or services). The survey also captures social capital aspects of the socialization of the poor in terms of generalized and specific trust, cooperation with other community members, and participation in formal and informal collective action.[1] The survey assesses the sense of control and optimism, the perception of the respondents' ability to influence government decision-making, and the satisfaction with services provided by local and national government. A parallel survey of local public officials carried out in the same localities helped relate the views of local officials on the effects and effectiveness of government activities to community perceptions of the quality of public service provision and other public interest issues.[2]

Quantitative study was complemented by qualitative analysis. Seventeen focus group sessions conducted with poor and average income inhabitants of urban and rural communities provided examples of interactions between community members and public and private service providers. A separate subset of focus sessions was conducted with poor urban and rural Roma groups and with public and private service providers.

Main Findings

The study finds the poor to be at a disadvantage in familial, social, and public networks.

Formal private transfers flow away from poor households. Consistent with the findings for other CEE countries, weak associational ties within private networks *de facto* act as strong closed networks catering to their immediate membership and demonstrating little altruistic interest in the poorer members of the community. This study shows that clubs and professional and special interest associations primarily channel resources to better-off households, who are more likely to be their members. At the same time, the poor, particularly the rural poor, contribute disproportionately to many organizations, particularly to church groups. This is consistent with data from some developed countries, where church related transfers were found to be regressive.[3]

Informal inter-household flows are income neutral. These results run counter to the economic literature on inter-household transactions, which finds the net effect of informal flows in developing countries to favor poorer and more vulnerable households and to act as means-tested public transfers. However, the finding is consistent with recent sociological studies of transitional economies noted above, which show post-socialist dislocation to cause rifts in informal ties, thereby diminishing access for the poor to the informal networks to which they once belonged.

A detailed block of questions, in the study, on types and channels of informal transactions among households revealed much more active participation of the population as a whole in informal transactions than is captured by traditional budget surveys. Ninety-seven per cent of respondents reported participating in informal gift giving and exchanges, with similar shares of poor and better-off households participating in informal inter-household transactions.

The reason for the low or negative net effect of informal inter-household transfers is not the paucity of transactions, but the prevalence of outflows over inflows for most types of informal transactions. Informal transfers as a share of total income before informal transactions are reported to constitute on average 8.5 per cent of household income for inflows and 12.3 per cent for outflows. A higher share of outflows for all income groups is attributed to three factors: 1) a high

---

1. Compared to the majority of budget household level surveys this study examines consistently both the income and the expenditure effects of informal transfers, looking at gift giving and exchanges symmetrically, both as a source of revenue for a household and as an expenditure item.

2. The questionnaires can be viewed at http://www.worldbank.org/romania/povertyassessment.

3. For contributions of the poor to religious charities in the US, see Verba etal. (1995). For a definition of progressive/regressive transfers, see footnote 3.

level of transfers from rural households in foodstuffs and financial assistance (from pensions and sale of agricultural output) of rural parents to adult urban children and other relatives; 2) the high price for poor households of remaining in networks including higher income households (the price of symbolic capital); and 3) the patterns of recollection, with respondents remembering the smallest gifts, exchanges and payments flowing out of the household (higher frequency, lower value of transactions), while recalling only the larger gifts, payments and exchanges flowing in (lower frequency, higher value).

The important difference captured in the study is the qualitative difference in types of transactions accessible to poorer and richer households. The poor are less likely to participate *in altruistic gift-giving* and more likely to engage in *reciprocal transactions*, such as exchanges of goods and services, as well as payments for minor services (minor repairs, child care, and tutoring).

About one half of all households are involved in informal lending. For the poor, lending and borrowing comes in the form of multiple transactions that are small in value, and help smooth consumption for a household anticipating monthly public assistance or public benefits transfers (pensions, minimum income assistance, and child allowances). This pattern graphically shows at the individual household level the interconnection of private and public flows as a single risk management system, with public assistance leveraged against informal flows from neighbors, friends, and sometimes relatives.

The poor have lower levels of trust in neighbors and other people in general. The poor are not as connected and have markedly fewer people they can rely on in solving pertinent life problems (health, legal, administrative, problems with the police, bank, assistance in getting a job). Lower levels of trust and participation translate into lower "dividends" from social capital, such as assistance in need and informal help with employment.

In this context *assistance from the government becomes particularly important.* Indeed, poor and rural households are more likely to trust both local and national government and be satisfied with services provided. This may be the result of lower expectations of the poorer and less educated population strata or it may reflect the high level of dependence on the government by those excluded from private networks. Hopefully, it is also the result of the effort and performance of local governments, particularly those in small rural areas where local administrators know most of their constituency personally and are more open to public scrutiny. The MIG programs, despite a number of flaws discussed in more detail below, appear to be well-targeted to poorer households with lower incomes, a high number of children, and fewer assets.

On balance, the evidence from this survey suggests that *poorer and rural households may suffer "triple exclusion." Not only do formal and informal market and inter-household activities favour rich and urban households, they also appear to have a more effective voice with respect to government services.* Households from the richest quintile and urban dwellers are more likely to be "civic activists"; attend public meetings, participate in protests, and alert the media to local problems. They are twice as likely as households in the poorest two quintiles to contact local officials about a public issue, and ten times as likely to contact national officials. Because of their higher incomes, they are also more capable of pursuing better public services through informal means. Richer households offer "gifts" to public officials more often to help resolve their problems.

At the community level, controlling for other variables, households living in localities with higher levels of civic activism (measured by an index of attending public meetings, participating in protests, alerting media to local problems, notifying the police or court of local problems) *receive higher MIG assistance,* which may point to the positive role of accountability of local governments in MIG allocations. Another important community level finding is that *poor communities have been found to be at a disadvantage in terms of access to fiscal transfers.* Poor households, particularly rural poor households, are more likely to live in areas that receive less earmarked and non-earmarked transfers from the central and county governments. All public transfers except for the national Minimum Income Guarantee program (MIG) are found to be regressive. Combined with lower levels of private support, a lower ability to self-organize, lower levels of public activism among the poor, and self-admitted higher dependence on state support these reduced flows may perpetuate the cycle of poverty and exclusion.

Policy Implications

The findings presented here have important policy implications at two levels. First, the study deepens our understanding of the *concrete role major social assistance programs* play in the livelihoods of the poor, specifically, the national social assistance program, MIG. MIG payments constitute a fairly small share of total income for the first quintile once all other income sources are taken into account (3.6 per cent), though this share increases quite substantially when the recipient households are factored out from the first *decile* (21.3 per cent of income for the 28 per-cent of recipient households in the sample), rather than the first *quintile*. However, if we take into account the anti-poor nature of other public transfers and the exclusion of the poor from informal public and private networks, the relevance of MIG payments in the livelihoods of poor households increases dramatically. The qualitative part of the study indicates that MIG is valued very highly by poor recipients, as it provides cash in hand at regular intervals and helps to leverage other transfers—informal lending, exchanges, and even ad hoc employment. At the same time, the study uncovered important institutional and organizational constraints to the improved targeting and cost-effectiveness of MIG flows. These include: 1) arbitrary allocation of MIG management resources and assessment of need by local government officials, 2) the need to finance a share of MIG-related expenditures from local budgets, which are particularly burdensome for poor and rural localities, and 3) the high costs of filing, information-gathering, and transportation faced by potential recipients in some areas. *The finding that MIG assistance is higher (controlling for income and other factors) in large localities, in localities with greater locally-raised revenues, and in localities with fewer Roma suggests that adjustments are needed to improve equal access to social assistance.*

At *the level of policy design*, findings of the study can contribute to improved conceptualization and development of *policymaking instruments and approaches that work*. The analysis shows that the poor live in a very distinct social environment. This environment affects their economic opportunities and coping strategies, in many ways defining particular channels through which the poor access social assistance and social protection programs. The challenge for the government is to incorporate this expanded understanding of how the poor live and interact with other households, private organizations (including private service providers; trade, labor and land/forest owners associations; the church), and local government into more readily accessible and effective social programs.

The finding that other public transfers are regressive at the locality level, and that the poor are less organized in voicing their discontent and working collectively for their rights should send a message to the government *to broaden its pro-poor approach to public transfers*.

To include the poorer constituency into both decision-making and service-providing networks, *local governments need to re-examine the way they interact with the poorer population*. The menu of possible procedural changes includes: 1) site visits to these areas followed by concrete community level actions, 2) specialized outreach programs, and 3) other efforts that include communities in the budgetary process and the evaluation of service provision. In other words, local governments must choose from a menu of practical empowerment mechanisms that have borne fruit in other parts of the world and adapt them to local realities and circumstances (Anderson 2002).

Finally, it is important to take into account ingrained traditions of interaction. Changes in social capital cannot be decreed or legislated. This study shows significant differences in the patterns of trust to communities, neighbors and the government as well as different propensity to cooperate among households residing in areas historically ruled by different empires (Habsburg vs. Ottoman). *Different traditions of public administration and different levels of trust and readiness for collective actions need to be taken into account when the government considers such issues as local governance reforms or de- vs. recentralization of service provision.*

The paper is structured as follows. The second chapter presents an overview of all income sources, concentrating on public and private transfers and their role in the income of poor households. The third chapter analyses the role of various informal inflows and outflows in the livelihoods of households from different income groups. The progressive/regressive nature of these transfers for the poor quintile is assessed.[4] The third chapter looks at maps of inter-household transfers in terms of: 1) the nature of relationships among transacting households, 2) the form of transactions (cash vs. in-kind), and 3) the geography of exchanges (same locality, other Romanian locality, other country). The fourth chapter discusses demographic, economic and social characteristics of households in relation to their net position as either donor or recipient of informal flows versus being uninvolved in informal transactions. Multivariate analysis is used to provide a more rigorous examination of the determinants of inter-household flows, such as vulnerability, access to public social flows, and participation in collective action. The fifth chapter examines the role of trust and collective action in the access of the poor to private and public flows. It assesses the relationship between the social capital endowment of a locality and such characteristics as ethnic diversity, the quality of public services, and the nature of local government. We note the tendency of local governments to provide better services to better organized, networked, and ethnically homogenous communities. It also points at ingrained historical nature of social capital, by relating trust to government and propensity to interact to imperial legacies (Habsburg vs. Ottoman legacies). The sixth chapter concludes with policy implications.

---

4. The progressive/regressive nature of transactions are used to identify the inequality-reducing or redistributive impact of social protection transfers. A transfer is *regressive* if the poorest groups receive a smaller share of program benefits than the share of the group in total consumption, i.e. when the poor benefit less relative to the rest of the population. A *progressive* transfer captures the opposite effect—where the poorest groups receive a larger share of program benefits than the share of the group in total consumption, i.e. when the poor benefit more relative to the rest of the population.

CHAPTER 2

SOURCES OF INCOME—AN OVERVIEW

The main difference in the structure of formal income sources between the poorest and other quintiles is that household income for the poorest quintile is dominated by transfers, while for all other quintiles officially recorded salary constitutes the most important source of income (Table 1). As expected, private business is far more important for household incomes in the highest quintile than for incomes of all other quintiles. As transfers in this analysis include both public and private flows, we will examine them in turn by category.

Public and Private Formal Transfers

Almost half of all income in the poorest quintile comes from formal transfers (Table 1). The most important part of public transfers are *social benefits*, which include old age and other pensions, scholarships, and child benefits. These benefits constitute 38 per cent of total net income for the poorest quintile, with similar shares of recipients from urban and rural households, as compared to 13.3 per cent of income for high-income households. Interestingly, pensioners report leveraging their pension in negotiations with potential employers, as this secure source of income makes them more attractive as workers that may require lower payment and lower benefits. Examples of exploitation were brought up in focus group sessions:

> Private employers want to hire pensioners . . . because, they say, I'll give them 1 million lei [US$30.25] as wages, then they have their 2 million lei [US$60.50] from their pension, and they will be happy.[5]
>
> —Average income resident, Breaza, urban

---

5. In 2002, the average exchange rate was 33,055.40 lei per US dollar.

TABLE I: NET TOTAL INCOME AVERAGE FOR 2002—BY NUMBER OF HOUSEHOLDS (2,590 HOUSEHOLDS)

Household Type		Formal Income (A) (1+2+3)	Formal Earned Income — Salary (1)	Private Business (2)	Net Formal Transfer (3) (a+b+c+d)	Public Social Benefits (a)	Public Social Assistance (b)	Other Transfers from Formal Public Sources (c)	Transfers from Formal Private Sources (d)	Informal Income (B) (f+g+h)	Informal Wages, Small Scale Agricultural Production and Leasing of Land (f)	Gift (g)	Exchange (h)	Other (C)	Total Income (A+B+C)
Q1	lei	19,817,781	6,811,427	802,348	12,204,006	9,703,371	901,023	1,512,935	86,677	3,087,173	7,357,483	-4,225,193	-45,117	2,341,668	25,246,622
	#HHs	482	130	19	463	423	133	220	14	518	515	483	333	214	518
Q2	lei	40,560,608	21,800,000	1,123,121	17,637,488	14,400,000	877,690	2,171,154	188,644	5,979,315	9,015,588	-2,968,139	-68,134	3,237,302	49,777,225
	#HHs	511	281	21	487	464	113	234	33	518	518	491	266	144	518
Q3	lei	58,340,592	33,800,000	1,443,353	23,097,239	18,000,000	749,699	3,690,069	657,471	6,735,959	8,914,560	-2,310,112	131,511	3,598,365	68,674,917
	#HHs	515	312	23	468	437	96	240	42	518	517	480	262	146	518
Q4	lei	73,047,540	43,800,000	2,180,385	27,067,154	21,000,000	932,212	4,601,375	533,567	9,455,096	11,811,848	-2,479,335	122,583	4,672,021	87,174,658
	#HHs	514	301	26	462	425	104	251	41	518	518	484	232	162	518
Q5	lei	135,014,316	67,600,000	24,300,000	43,114,316	22,400,000	1,654,751	15,600,000	3,459,565	22,285,632	19,388,538	2,424,584	472,510	11,957,524	169,257,472
	#HHs	513	298	69	448	397	101	289	40	518	518	485	229	166	518
Total	lei	65,391,619	34,800,000	5,966,436	24,625,183	17,100,000	1,022,914	5,517,518	984,751	9,500,994	11,290,664	-1,912,200	122,530	5,152,812	80,045,425
	#HHs	2,535	1,322	158	2,328	2,146	547	1234	170	2592	2,586	2,425	1322	779	2,592
Q1	% lei	78.5%	26.8%	3.2%	48.3%	38.4%	3.6%	6.0%	0.3%	12.2%	29.1%	-16.7%	-0.2%	9.3%	100.0%
	%HHs	93.1%	25.1%	3.7%	89.6%	81.7%	25.7%	42.5%	2.7%	100.0%	99.4%	93.2%	64.3%	41.3%	100.0%
Q2	% lei	81.5%	43.8%	2.5%	35.4%	28.9%	1.8%	4.4%	0.4%	12.0%	18.1%	-6.0%	-0.1%	6.5%	100.0%
	%HHs	98.6%	54.2%	4.1%	94.0%	89.4%	21.8%	45.2%	6.4%	100.0%	100.0%	94.8%	51.4%	27.8%	100.0%
Q3	% lei	85.0%	49.2%	2.1%	33.6%	26.2%	1.1%	5.4%	1.0%	9.8%	13.0%	-3.4%	0.2%	5.2%	100.0%
	%HHs	99.4%	60.2%	4.4%	90.3%	84.4%	18.5%	46.3%	8.1%	100.0%	99.8%	92.7%	50.6%	28.2%	100.0%
Q4	% lei	83.8%	50.2%	2.5%	31.0%	24.1%	1.1%	5.3%	0.6%	10.8%	13.5%	-2.8%	0.1%	5.4%	100.0%
	%HHs	99.2%	58.1%	5.0%	89.2%	82.0%	20.1%	48.5%	7.9%	100.0%	100.0%	93.4%	44.8%	31.3%	100.0%
Q5	% lei	79.8%	39.9%	14.4%	28.4%	13.2%	1.0%	9.2%	2.0%	13.2%	11.5%	1.4%	0.3%	7.1%	100.0%
	%HHs	99.0%	57.5%	13.3%	86.5%	76.6%	19.5%	55.8%	7.7%	100.0%	100.0%	93.6%	44.2%	32.0%	100.0%
Total	% lei	81.7%	43.5%	7.5%	30.8%	21.4%	1.3%	6.9%	1.2%	11.9%	14.1%	-2.4%	0.2%	6.4%	100.0%
	%HHs	97.8%	51.0%	6.1%	89.8%	82.8%	21.1%	47.6%	6.6%	100.0%	99.8%	93.6%	51.0%	30.1%	100.0%

Formal Transfer by Category; Informal Income by Category / Informal Inter Household Transfers

Formal Income: salary, income through civil convention/ collaboration contract, independent authorized non/agricultural activities, State old age pension, Veteran or disability pension, CAP pension, scholarships, child benefits, other social payments, income from investments, savings, rent on other properties, income from business profit, formal public and private assistance (such as social allowances, emergency relief, etc.) *Formal Transfers:* state old age pension + veteran pension or disability pension + CAP pension + scholarship + child benefits + other social payments + formal public and private assistance (such as social allowances, emergency relief, etc.) *Public Social Benefit:* State old age pension, Veteran or disability pension, CAP pension, scholarships, child benefits; *Public Social Assistance:* social allowances, emergency relief, allowances for the wives of conscripts, subsidies for heating dwellings connected to the public heating system, subsidies for heating by fuel, firewood and/or coal; *Other Transfers from Formal Public Sources:* Formal public assistance from the local council, police, prefect's office, National Government, City Hall, Communal administration agency, and public hospitals and schools; subventions for medical assistance (ie surgery); subsidies for agricultural services; subsidized ticket for traveling by rail; subsidized loans for building/ buying a house; *Transfers from Formal Private Sources:* Formal private assistance from associations such as the Village/Neighborhood committee and Parents committee, and private schools and hospitals + money from sponsors + donations; *Informal Income Total:* daily wages, small scale agricultural production, leasing of land, others, net gift and donations, net exchanges of services, payments; *Earning from Agriculture and informal daily wages:* income from daily work or temporary incomes, income from household agricultural production, yearly self- consumption; *Income from Rent and Leasing of Land:* income for land rented for use, income for land leased to others; *Gift:* gift inflow-gift outflow; *Net exchange:* exchange of similar and different services; *Other informal sources:* payment inflow, money from relatives who work temporarily in another country, other sources.

Source: Public/Private Transfers and Social Capital Survey, World Bank, 2003.

Note: In 2002, the average exchange rate was 333,055.40 lei per US dollar.

Broader access of the elderly to social benefits often turns them into providers for their younger relatives:

> I have a daughter and a son-in-law, and two nieces, and their income is only 1.6M lei. There are four of them in their family . . . If it wasn't for myself and my wife, and for our pensions, how would they manage? So we, the elderly, choose to help them. Because, thanks be to God, I don't need anything fancy, I have everything I need. But the young people, they are truly in a dire situation.
>
> —Low income respondent, Alunis, rural

> Now my only source of support is my father's pension. There are five of us in our family, and we all live off my father's pension.
>
> —Low income respondent, Alunis, rural

Social assistance, which includes social allowances, emergency relief, and different heating compensations, constitutes 3.6 per cent of income for the poorest quintile, is available to 25.7 per cent of households from the poorest quintile and is progressive (Table 1). More urban poor households (35.1 per cent) receive social assistance than their rural counterparts (21.8 per cent; see Tables A1a and A1b in Appendix A). For the poorest decile the importance of social assistance is more dramatic—28 per cent of households in this decile receive social assistance. For recipient households in the poorest decile social assistance constitutes 21.3 per cent of total income. In comparison, 23.3 per cent of households from the second decile, receive only 8.4 per cent of total formal income from social assistance.

Recipients of social assistance (MIG) consider it to be a vital part of their income, as assistance is received at regular intervals and represents "cash in hand" for cash-strapped households. Focus group respondents indicated that the guaranteed income enabled them to borrow small sums of money or products from neighbors, relatives, and food stores, thereby smoothing consumption in times of hardship:

> We have neighbors, relatives who can lend some things to us. There are also the elderly who receive pensions, and we sometimes go to them, and they lend us money. When we receive the (child) allocation or social aid, we return the money we borrowed. (. . .) Because if you don't repay your loan, no one will lend you any money in the future.
>
> —Low income respondents, Nereju, rural

> R1: Too little help! We don't really help each other! Only when we come to the store and they give us things. But even here you know you must bring money to pay for these things.
> R2: We certainly know we must bring the money!
> R2: And even at the store, when do you know that you can come and buy things? It is only when you know your (social) aid is coming, that you will get some money.
>
> —Roma, low income respondents, Alunis, rural

At the same time, social assistance recipients and other low income focus group respondents complained about difficulties in accessing public assistance due to four main factors: 1) poor access to information describing the documentation needed to receive aid and various eligibility criteria, 2) the dismissive attitudes of local officials, 3) the high costs for filing documentation, and 4) the inability of poorer localities to cope with their social assistance mandates.

Poor access to information, dismissive attitude:
> There is a new social aid law, and for newborns up to the age of six months you get 750,000 lei [US$22.69]. The newspapers say so. When I went to ask about this, they said they had not heard about it, that I should go talk to Adrian Năstase [Prime Minister of Romania].
>
> —Roma, low income respondents, Focşani, urban

Lack of awareness:

I have noticed that plenty of these people (the poor, mainly) have almost never made any attempt, or they simply did not know how to apply for social aid from County hall. I know a few examples of individuals who were supposed to receive such benefits. They even told me that they went there, but were not given any help in this respect. So this is the problem. Such people occupy the last position on the social scale, if I may say so. If they were to benefit from social aid, they would implicitly qualify for free medical assistance. A large majority of them did not know anything about this, others had not received any guidance from City Hall, that is they were misinformed.

—Physician, Breaza, urban

Arbitrariness of local officials:

If one owned a horse, for example, or a wagon, they would not give you social aid! If you owned a Persian carpet (i.e., of good quality) in your house they wouldn't give you social aid either. Also, if you own a television set, you don't get any aid! But, one would think that perhaps, a 50-year old person, after 20 or so years of being married, may have been able to accumulate a few things/or, to accomplish something.

—Roma, low income respondent, Alunis, urban

Costs of accessing services:

Last year, they were very disrespectful towards me and my wife. They asked her to go to the notary and certify a personal income statement, which cost 85,000 lei [US$2.57]. The costs for obtaining documentation are very high.

—Low income respondents, Galati, urban

Inability of poorer localities to cope with social assistance mandates:

There are decisions taken by the Government, but they are applied at the local level. They give social help to those people with income below a certain level, for example. The money should come from the local budget, but the local budget doesn't have enough money. They provided social assistants for people with disabilities. These assistants are employees. First they were paid by the Ministry of Labor. After that, they asked the local governments to pay 25 percent. In the next year they asked them to pay 50 percent. Now the local governments must pay 100 percent of the social assistants' salaries. This costs the local government about 3 billion lei [US$90,756.73]. And now we have reached the point where the local government doesn't even have enough money to repair a hole in the road.

—Local councilor, Breaza

I'm speaking about the local budgets of the villages, which are extremely small. I know villages that can hardly cover their operating costs. Among the material services provided, the Minimum Income Guarantee (MIG) is the most affected, because there are not enough funds. I have no specific data with me, but as far as I know, there were more than twenty thousand demands. These were only partially covered. And even those that were approved, many of them were not paid in full.

—Public service provider, Targu Mures

Another category of *public transfers* are *payments made by local government* (city hall, local council, prefecture, specialized national agencies), and *by public service providers* (hospitals, schools, kindergartens). These transfers include public assistance for high cost medical emergencies, public medical insurance, and ad hoc assistance for education; railway ticket subsidies for pensioners, veterans, and students; agricultural subsidies; and subsidized loans for the purchase of primary residence. These are important flows that reach 47.6 per cent of the sample (1,234 households; Table 1). Public transfers constitute 6.4 per cent of total income for the poorest quintile; 4.6 per cent for the second quintile; and 10 per cent of total income for the highest income quintile, demonstrating greater importance of these transfers for the incomes of richer households (Table 1).

Separating these transfers into assistance from public service providers (assistance with health emergencies, childcare, and education), and other public transfers from local or national

TABLE 2: TRANSFERS FROM PUBLIC SERVICE PROVIDING INSTITUTIONS AND FROM PUBLIC ASSISTANCE PROGRAMS, BY QUINTILE

	Number of Households Receiving Transfers from Public Service Providers	Share of All Households Receiving	Number of Households Receiving Transfers from Other Public Programs	Share of All Households Receiving
Quintile 1	98	19.0%	163	16.1%
Quintile 2	95	18.4%	188	18.6%
Quintile 3	91	17.7%	196	19.3%
Quintile 4	107	20.8%	208	20.5%
Quintile 5	104	20.2%	258	25.5%
Total	**515**	**100.0%**	**1,013**	**100.0%**

Source: Public/Private Transfers and Social Capital Survey, World Bank, 2003.

government (subsidized investments, agricultural subsidies, and assistance for transportation) helps discern the following divergent patterns (Table 2 and 2a). Assistance from public service providers is more progressive, and reaches a comparable number of households in different income quintiles, while other public transfers are highly regressive, with more high income households receiving these transfers both in absolute terms and as a share of income.

Formal Private Social Flows

Formal private networks include associations such as trade unions, church groups, parent committees, neighborhood associations, agricultural associations, professional associations, and NGOs. Overall, active membership in these organizations is fairly high, as 1,302 households, or 49.3 per cent of the sample, report being members of at least one of these groups. Poor households report lower associational membership than more well-to-do households. 33 per cent of households from the poorest quintile report membership in an association compared to 60.5 per cent for the highest income quintile. The highest overall membership is reported for Trade and Labor Unions (29.7 per cent of all associated members), Owners' Associations (24.0 per cent of associated members), and Agricultural Societies (20.5 per cent; Table 3). Of these three, Trade and Labor Unions have the lowest membership among the poorer quintile (around 4 per cent of households) and Agricultural Societies the highest (11.43 per cent of these households). The latter is comparable to membership from the second through fourth quintiles and is 30 per cent higher than membership from the highest income quintile.

On average, formal private associations do not seem oriented towards assisting the poor. Both cash and in-kind payments and services are provided to average and higher income households, who are more likely to be their members, and are regressive as a share of household income. The highest income quintile receives 2 per cent of total income from private associations, while the poorest quintile gets only 0.3 per cent of income from these transfers (Table 1). Socially vulnerable groups, such as female-headed households receive a significantly lower number of transfers than non-female headed households. Pensioners do not get significantly more assistance than other household groups. The poor report being isolated from those groups that were previously open to them:

> Before, people were not layered as such, in these categories. Now the Forest Association also associates itself only with the rich, and everyone else is excluded. This is how our world is nowadays.
> —Average income respondents, Nereju, rural

TABLE 2A: TRANSFERS FROM PUBLIC SERVICE PROVIDING INSTITUTIONS AND FROM PUBLIC ASSISTANCE PROGRAMS, BY QUINTILE

Variable	Average Transfers from Public Service Providers (in lei)	As a Share of the Transfer	As a Share of Income before the Transfer	Average Transfers from Other Public Programs (in lei)	As a Share of the Transfer	As a Share of Income before the Transfer
Quintile 1	474,786	9.3%	2.00%	1,038,149	4.6%	4.38%
Quintile 2	559,550	10.9%	1.17%	1,611,604	7.2%	3.37%
Quintile 3	771,830	15.1%	1.19%	2,918,239	13.0%	4.49%
Quintile 4	1,108,184	21.6%	1.34%	3,493,191	15.6%	4.23%
Quintile 5	2,332,030	45.5%	1.52%	13,267,970	59.1%	8.67%
All households	**1,025,157**	**100%**	**1.38%**	**4,492,361**	**100%**	**6.04%**

Source: Public/Private Transfers and Social Capital Survey, World Bank, 2003.

TABLE 3: MEMBERSHIP OF HOUSEHOLD MEMBERS IN ORGANIZATIONS

Organization	Size of Member Households (as % of the sample)
Trade Union or Labor Union	29.7%
Owners' association	24.0%
Agricultural society with legal personality	20.5%
Parents' committee	18.0%
Church committee or other forms of collective church coordination	16.5%
Political party	15.2%
Professional Association	12.4%
Family-Type Agricultural Association	10.8%
Other Associations	10.3%
Artists' /sports association	9.6%
Traders or Business Association	8.7%
Money rotating system	8.6%
NGO or civic group	7.1%

Source: Public/Private Transfers and Social Capital Survey, World Bank, 2003.

> It is very hard! I asked someone I knew if I could borrow his tractor, which I used to bring home some wood for heating. Before, the communa used to give us wood, that was actually the reason why the communa owned the woods. And they used to write down the names of all the poor people in a table, and sell it to them for a reduced price; they used to chop the wood in smaller pieces, measure it in cubic meters, then give it to the poor, so that it would be enough (for everyone) . . .
> —Low income respondent, Alunis, rural

At the same time, the poor are active contributors to private associations—75 per cent of households from the poorest quintile contribute to different public groups, as opposed to 77 percent from the highest income quintile (Table 4).

The church, through church groups, and *the school*, through parent committees, are the largest recipients of contributions (Table A4a in Appendix A). 63 per cent of the sample contributes to the church, while the next biggest recipient—the parent's committee—receives contributions from only 13 per cent of the sample. While richer households are more often represented in church committees, the poor (particularly the rural poor) are the most active contributors to church causes (Table 4b and 4c). The vulnerable groups are equally likely to contribute to church causes (Table 4d). There is no indication that churches distribute more support to vulnerable households (female-headed households and pensioners) than to average households.

Furthermore, the poor, specifically those in Roma communities, report high payments for religious rites and little support from local clergy. For the Roma these costs are reportedly aggravated by discrimination.

TABLE 4: CONTRIBUTIONS TO PRIVATE ORGANIZATIONS, BY QUINTILE

Variable	Total			Urban			Rural		
	Number	Mean (Lei)	As a share of income	Number	Mean (Lei)	As a share of income	Number	Mean (Lei)	As a share of income
Quintile 1	390	706,861	2.8%	93	768,752	2.7%	297	687,480	2.8%
Quintile 2	388	783,823	1.5%	176	714,326	1.2%	212	841,518	1.9%
Quintile 3	384	824,964	1.2%	219	656,971	0.9%	165	1,047,937	1.6%
Quintile 4	390	942,682	1.1%	281	972,354	1.0%	109	866,189	1.1%
Quintile 5	397	1,105,023	0.6%	296	1,177,137	0.6%	101	893,677	0.6%
All households	1949	873,743	1.0%	1065	903,996	0.9%	884	837,295	1.5%

Source: Public/Private Transfers and Social Capital, World Bank, 2003.

TABLE 4B: MEMBERSHIP IN CHURCH COMMITTEES

Church Committee or Other Forms of Collective Church Coordination	
Quintile 1	6.8%
Quintile 2	7.6%
Quintile 3	8.4%
Quintile 4	10.6%
Quintile 5	8.5%

Source: Public/Private Transfers and Social Capital, World Bank, 2003.

TABLE 4C: CONTRIBUTIONS TO CHURCH ACTIVITIES

	Total		Urban		Rural	
Variable	# of HHs	Percentage of quintile	# of HHs	Percentage of quintile	# of HHs	Percentage of quintile
Quintile 1	363	68,8%	71	47,0%	292	77,5%
Quintile 2	348	66,0%	144	53,9%	204	78,5%
Quintile 3	335	63,7%	183	54,5%	152	80,0%
Quintile 4	345	65,3%	225	58,8%	120	82,8%
Quintile 5	323	61,1%	239	55,7%	84	84,0%
All HHs	1,714	65,0%	862	55,0%	852	79,5%

Source: Public/Private Transfers and Social Capital, World Bank, 2003.

TABLE 4D: CONTRIBUTIONS TO CHURCH COMMITTEES AND ACTIVITIES, BY URBAN/RURAL AND VULNERABILITY

Variable	Number	Percent	Variable	Number	Percent	Variable	Number	Percent
Urban	862	55.0	Female head	280	65.7	Pensioner	533	66.2
Rural	852	79.5	Non-female head	1,434	64.8	Non-Pensioner	1181	64.4

Source: Public/Private Transfers and Social Capital, World Bank, 2003.

The Church! That's another problem. Well, all the Roma here in the communa are Orthodox. For example, at Easter the priest goes around to everyone's home to sprinkle their house with holy water. I owe the priest some money, and was not able to pay him back. The holidays came and went . . . and the priest did not stop by at all! He went to the neighboring houses, and he did not even bother to stop by to ask me how I was doing, or if I wanted him to bless my house.(. . .)If you have money, you pay the priest, if you don't, he doesn't stop by, he doesn't care about you.

—Roma, low income respondents, Alunis, urban

We are discriminated against from all sides. All the local leaders discriminate against us. My little girl was sick and I asked the priest to please baptize her. He said, until you make your payment, I won't baptize her!

—Roma, low income respondents, Alunis, urban

TABLE 5: FLOWS FROM PRIVATE BUSINESSES AND PRIVATE SERVICE PROVIDERS

Variable	Transfers from Private Businesses			Transfers from Private Service Providers		
	N	Mean (lei)	As a share of income	N	Mean (lei)	As a share of income
Q1	14	86,677	0.30%	0	0	0.00%
Q2	28	175,353	0.40%	7	13,291	0.03%
Q3	38	584,563	0.90%	11	72,908	0.11%
Q4	31	521,567	0.60%	3	12,000	0.01%
Q5	33	3,390,530	2.00%	7	69,035	0.04%
Total	144	956,829	1.20%	28	27,922	0.03%

Source: Public/Private Transfers and Social Capital Survey, World Bank, 2003.

Formal Private Organizations

Both private service providers and private institutional economic actors provide some assistance to a closed group of employees, clients, and associates. These transfers are also highly regressive, with the highest income quintile receiving more assistance from formal private institutional actors—most likely their employers—as well as from private service providers (Table 5). Philanthropic flows do not register as significant in this sample.

To conclude, official public flows form a very important source of income for poorer households, the most important being social benefits and targeted social assistance. Disturbingly, testimonials single out the high cost of accessing social assistance in some localities, the arbitrary nature of resource allocation by local officials, the inability of poorer localities to fund the local share of expenses, and discrimination against the Roma by leaders and elite groups of the community (for a more detailed multivariate analysis of social and fiscal determinants of MIG flows see chapter 5). At the same time, it is important to note that other public flows are not pro-poor by nature. Formal private flows are highly regressive, pointing to the closed non-altruistic nature of the newly formed interest groups and associations. At present, the poor do not benefit from non-government-sponsored formal transfers, which makes them even more dependent on the state for assistance.

Informal Income

Informal income is vital for both urban and rural poor households. These flows include: 1) earnings from informal wages, small scale agricultural production and leasing of land; 2) inter-household gift giving; and 3) exchanges.[6]

All households in the sample participate in some type of informal transactions. 12.2 per cent of total income in the poorest quintile comes from informal sources. The lowest share of informal income is 9.8 per cent for quintile 3, and the highest share is 13.2 per cent for the highest income quintile (Table 1).

Patterns of formal and informal flows differ for rural and urban populations. The rural population receives more than one third of its total income from informal wages, small scale

---

6. Since there is no prior tradition of netting out payments in income calculations, informal payments in Table 1 are included as payment inflows and added to "other sources of income." For a more detailed analysis of informal payments see Chapter 3 on inter-household transfers.

agricultural production, and land leasing, while the share of these items is only 16.2 per cent for the urban poor (Table A1a and A1b, Appendix A).

Small scale private plot production allows the rural poor to feed their families from own agricultural production and to sell this produce at local markets. Agricultural seasonal work is also an important source of income for rural landless households. In urban areas, service day jobs are reported to be important for the survival of poor households, though the poor—the poor Roma in particular—report that it is increasingly difficult to find odd jobs (cleaning, carpentry, etc.) in towns, partly because of the decrease in solidarity within ethnic groups and networks of relatives:

Low wages for odd service jobs
> We work a full day for only 20,000 lei [US$0.60]. It is very difficult today to raise three children. They (the relatives) all have their own companies, but they will not hire us.
> —Female, low income respondent, Breaza, urban

> Seeds are the major source of income. We sell seeds. We wash, whitewash; I have sometimes earned 35,000 [US$1.06] a day, and could not do anything with this money . . . Seasonal work . . . And this if we find offers for such jobs. When Easter comes, we work (. . .) We work wherever we are offered jobs. I know old acquaintances who offer me jobs typically for one day only. We also find out about other jobs from newspapers.
> —Roma, low income respondent, Focşani, urban

Both the household level survey and focus group testimonials demonstrate that it is easier to get ad hoc informal jobs in rural areas. There is evidence of self-organization of the poor in teams of day laborers:

> Those who are poor, who lack any assets, they have a hard time making ends meet. They make a living by working as day laborers, mainly in agriculture. They may also raise animals. Sometimes they form teams and go throughout the countryside looking for work (in agriculture, on the fields). They don't earn a lot of money. They typically come back with agricultural produce such as corn or money. Enough to cover some basic life necessities, but nothing more.
> —President of Nereju Community Organization, Nereju, rural

Participants of poor Roma focus groups singled out summer agricultural employment as a particularly vital source of income:

> Everyone, everyone goes to work for food, as day laborers. We find employment, day by day, but not now, only in the summertime . . . In the wintertime you die of starvation. In the summertime, you can manage. The best time period for the Roma here is in the summer, when you can breathe a little, when we go to Gheorgheni and pick blueberries and raspberries . . .
> —Low income respondents, Alunis, rural

Because the study is more focused on formal and informal social transfers and social solidarity within open and closed networks, we do not concentrate on incomes sources from informal employment, and instead will turn to informal inter-household transfers.

CHAPTER 3

INFORMAL INTER-HOUSEHOLD FLOWS

The next informal source of income in importance is net informal inter-household transfers. These include: 1) altruistic gifts presented to and received from other households, and 2) exchanges of goods and services between households. In total household income net gifts (inflows minus outflows) are negative for all categories of households but the richest quintile. Net exchanges are also negative for poor rural households and for the second quintile of urban households (Table A1a and A1b in Appendix A). We now analyze informal flows in more detail, in order to: 1) assess the role of informal incomes in the livelihoods of poor households; 2) determine the likelihood of receiving and transferring resources to other households; and 3) construct a map that relates the nature and geography of informal transfers to household income, characteristics, and social environment.

Informal Inter-household Flows by Category

Informal flows are found to be substantial and widespread. Households in all income categories participate extensively in informal inter-household transfers (almost 97 per cent of all sampled households). Flows among households are significant when measured as a fraction of household income before inter-household transfers. Gross informal outflows equal 12.3 per cent and gross informal inflows equal 8.5 per cent of net income before inter-household transfers. Not surprisingly, these shares are higher for inflows and outflows for the poorest quintile, 17.8 and 17.6 per cent respectively. If we compare these income shares to MIG-related transfers, we will see that informal gift-giving flows in absolute terms are 5 times greater than MIG-related transfers! This comparison brings out again the importance of informal flows in the livelihoods of Romanian households in general and poor households in particular.

TABLE 6A: TOTAL INTER-HOUSEHOLD TRANSACTIONS OUTFLOWS (IN LEI AND PERCENTAGES)

Quintile	Inter-household Transaction	Gift	Payment	Exchange	Income before Inter-household Transaction
Q1	4,900,463	2,834,802	1,122,035	943,626	27,600,000
Q2	7,067,152	4,738,569	1,677,287	651,296	52,400,000
Q3	7,673,685	5,180,584	1,912,508	580,593	71,000,000
Q4	10,351,711	6,829,662	2,737,056	784,993	88,300,000
Q5	20,368,958	13,300,000	5,612,488	1,456,470	170,000,000
All HHs	10,070,846	6,575,175	2,612,275	883,396	81,900,000
As a Share of Total Inter-household Transactions					
Q1	100%	57.8%	22.9%	19.3%	
Q2	100%	67.1%	23.7%	9.2%	
Q3	100%	67.5%	24.9%	7.6%	
Q4	100%	66.0%	26.4%	7.6%	
Q5	100%	65.3%	27.6%	7.2%	
All HHs	100%	65.3%	25.9%	8.8%	
As a Share of a Particular Inter-household Transaction, by Quintile					
Q1	9.7%	8.6%	8.6%	21.4%	6.7%
Q2	14.0%	14.4%	12.8%	14.7%	12.8%
Q3	15.2%	15.8%	14.6%	13.1%	17.3%
Q4	20.6%	20.8%	21.0%	17.8%	21.6%
Q5	40.5%	40.5%	43.0%	33.0%	41.5%
All HHs	100.0%	100.0%	100.0%	100.0%	100.0%
As a Share of Total Income before a Particular Inter-household Transaction					
Q1	17.8%	10.3%	4.1%	3.4%	
Q2	13.5%	9.0%	3.2%	1.2%	
Q3	10.8%	7.3%	2.7%	0.8%	
Q4	11.7%	7.7%	3.1%	0.9%	
Q5	12.0%	7.8%	3.3%	0.9%	
All HHs	12.3%	8.0%	3.2%	1.1%	

Source: Public/Private Transfers and Social Capital, World Bank, 2003.

Gross transfers sent are about one third higher than the transfers received. This trend has already been noted among poor households in Romania in a study of extreme poverty.[7] The reason may be, as is borne by the data, that respondents recall the smallest gifts and loans extended to other households (the average value of outflows is smaller than the average value of inflows), and only the few and more significant contributions they have received themselves (the frequency of inflows is lower than the frequency of outflows). Similar perceptions were captured in focus group testimonials:

> The neighbors won't help me anymore, everybody minds his own business. If I ask for a cabbage he says that he doesn't have any. If anybody were to ask me for anything, I would give it to them for free.

> —Low income person, Breaza, urban

---

7. "It is a proven fact that the poor underestimate the help they receive and overestimate the help they offer" (Stanculescu and Berevoescu, forthcoming).

TABLE 6B: TOTAL INTER-HOUSEHOLD TRANSACTIONS INFLOWS (IN LEI AND PERCENTAGES)

Quintile	Inter-household Transaction	Gift	Payment	Exchange	Income before Inter-household Transaction
Q1	4,860,970	2,382,542	1,426,012	1,052,416	27,600,000
Q2	4,879,986	3,032,865	1,108,693	738,428	52,400,000
Q3	5,443,322	3,189,966	1,428,305	825,051	71,000,000
Q4	7,276,531	5,194,846	1,119,909	961,776	88,300,000
Q5	12,315,270	9,108,721	1,754,592	1,451,957	170,000,000
All HHs	6,955,216	4,581,788	1,367,502	1,005,926	81,900,000
As a Share of Total Inter-household Transactions					
Q1	100%	49.0%	29.3%	21.7%	
Q2	100%	62.1%	22.7%	15.1%	
Q3	100%	58.6%	26.2%	15.2%	
Q4	100%	71.4%	15.4%	13.2%	
Q5	100%	74.0%	14.2%	11.8%	
All HHs	100%	65.9%	19.7%	14.5%	
As a Share of a Particular Inter-household Transaction, by Quintile					
Q1	14.0%	10.4%	20.9%	20.9%	6.7%
Q2	14.0%	13.2%	16.2%	14.7%	12.8%
Q3	15.7%	13.9%	20.9%	16.4%	17.3%
Q4	20.9%	22.7%	16.4%	19.1%	21.6%
Q5	35.4%	39.8%	25.7%	28.9%	41.5%
All HHs	100.0%	100.0%	100.0%	100.0%	100.0%
As a Share of Total Income before a Particular Inter-household Transaction					
Q1	17.6%	8.6%	5.2%	3.8%	
Q2	9.3%	5.8%	2.1%	1.4%	
Q3	7.7%	4.5%	2.0%	1.2%	
Q4	8.2%	5.9%	1.3%	1.1%	
Q5	7.2%	5.4%	1.0%	0.9%	
All HHs	8.5%	5.6%	1.7%	1.2%	

Source: Public/Private Transfers and Social Capital, World Bank, 2003.

Another outstanding feature of this study is that the net effect of inter-household transfers is income neutral (Table 7). The results are similar for urban and rural households, and are not reported here.

The finding that inter-household transfers are income neutral runs counter to the results reported in related literature where inter-household transfers behave like means-tested public transfers and flow from the rich to the poor (Cox etal. 1996, Jimenez etal. 2001, Cox 2002). This outcome can be attributed to the more detailed nature of inter-household transactions mentioned above as well as to the particular configuration of interactions among households in post-socialist countries in general and in Romania in particular. It is also consistent with sociologists' findings on patterns of informal transactions in post-Socialist countries. Social ties are found to be built over time, to depend upon trust, and to require maintenance. The poor lack these resourcesand are often excluded (Pahl 1988, Morris and Irwin 1992). The situation seems to be exacerbated by post-Socialist dislocation on the one hand, in which old personal ties are strained

TABLE 7: INTER-HOUSEHOLD TRANSFERS AND INEQUALITY (IN LEI AND PERCENTAGES)

Variable	Income before Inter-household Transfer	Share	Income after Inter-household Transfer	Share
Decile 1	19,800,000	2.4%	19,300,000	2.4%
Decile 2	35,300,000	4.3%	34,900,000	4.4%
Decile 3	49,200,000	6.0%	47,300,000	5.9%
Decile 4	55,600,000	6.8%	54,100,000	6.8%
Decile 5	70,600,000	8.6%	68,400,000	8.6%
Decile 6	71,300,000	8.7%	69,500,000	8.7%
Decile 7	85,000,000	10.4%	82,600,000	10.3%
Decile 8	91,500,000	11.2%	90,600,000	11.3%
Decile 9	114,000,000	13.9%	113,000,000	14.1%
Decile 10	226,000,000	27.6%	219,000,000	27.4%
Quintile 1	27,550,000	6.7%	27,100,000	6.8%
Quintile 2	52,400,000	12.8%	50,700,000	12.7%
Quintile 3	70,950,000	17.3%	68,950,000	17.3%
Quintile 4	88,250,000	21.6%	86,800,000	21.6%
Quintile 5	170,000,000	41.5%	166,000,000	41.5%

Source: Public/Private Transfers and Social Capital, World Bank, 2003.

by newly-developed income inequality. On the other hand, functional informal ties based on the ability to obtain things in a shortage economy have been rendered useless by the advent of the market economy (Wedel 1986, Ledeneva 1998).

Focus group testimonials help identify some particular characteristics of informal outflows from poorer households. These are: 1) the disproportionate transfers to children made by poor rural parents in the form of agricultural produce or income from selling agricultural output produced on small plots, and 2) the high price paid by the poor for remaining in reciprocal networks.

Transfers to children:

> My daughter is in college. I raise a pig for them, every month I give them 40–50 eggs, I give them 500,000 – 1M lei because I feel pity for them.
> —Average income respondent, Alunis, rural

High cost of remaining in networks:

> If you cannot rise up to a certain level, you are pushed aside.
> Q: What does it mean, "to be pushed aside?"
> You cannot access their circles. They have many cars, and they have a lot of money.
> —Average income respondents, Alunis, urban

On the positive side, while summarily informal transactions are income neutral, some types of inter-household transactions appear progressive (Table 8).[8]

The most popular form of transaction is *gift giving* with 93.6 per cent of households exchanging gifts. Gift giving transactions are the highest in value among all inter-household transfers and are mildly progressive. Rural poor households perceive themselves as net givers, while urban poor households see themselves as net receivers of gifts. This pattern is consistent with the

---

8. For the definition of progressive/regressive transactions, see footnote 3.

TABLE 8: NET INFORMAL INTER-HOUSEHOLD TRANSACTIONS, BY CATEGORY

Household Type		Net Informal Inter-household Transactions	Gift	Payment	Exchanges	Total Income before Inter-household Transactions
Q1	lei	−39,493	−452,260	303,977	108,790	27,600,000
	# of HHs	504	482	338	325	518
Q2	lei	−2,243,663	−1,705,705	−568,594	87,133	52,400,000
	# of HHs	506	492	288	272	518
Q3	lei	−2,391,444	−1,990,617	−484,204	244,458	71,000,000
	# of HHs	496	481	273	247	518
Q4	lei	−3,084,466	−1,634,816	−1,617,147	176,783	88,300,000
	# of HHs	498	484	244	242	518
Q5	lei	−8,070,967	−4,183,539	−3,857,896	−4,513	170,000,000
	# of HHs	498	484	266	234	518
All HHs	lei	−3,164,701	−1,993,387	−1,244,773	122,530	81,900,000
	# of HHs	2,502	2,423	1,409	1,320	2590
As a Share of each Inter-household Transactions						
Q1	% lei	0.2%	4.5%	−4.9%	17.8%	6.7%
	% of HHs	20.1%	19.9%	24.0%	25.5%	20.0%
Q2	% lei	14.2%	17.1%	9.1%	14.2%	12.8%
	% of HHs	20.2%	20.3%	20.4%	20.1%	20.0%
Q3	% lei	15.1%	20.0%	7.8%	39.9%	17.3%
	% of HHs	19.8%	19.9%	19.4%	19.8%	20.0%
Q4	% lei	19.5%	16.4%	26.0%	28.9%	21.6%
	% of HHs	19.9%	20.0%	17.3%	17.6%	20.0%
Q5	% lei	51.0%	42.0%	62.0%	−0.7%	41.5%
	% of HHs	19.9%	20.0%	18.9%	17.3%	20.0%
All HHs	% lei	100%	100%	100%	100%	100%
	% of HHs	100%	100%	100%	100%	100%
As a Share of Total Income before a Particular Inter-household Transactions						
Q1	% lei	−0.1%	−1.6%	1.1%	0.4%	100%
	% of HHs	97.3%	93.1%	65.3%	62.7%	100%
Q2	% lei	−4.3%	−3.3%	−1.1%	0.2%	100%
	% of HHs	97.7%	95.0%	55.6%	52.5%	100%
Q3	% lei	−3.4%	−2.8%	−0.7%	0.3%	100%
	% of HHs	95.8%	92.9%	52.7%	47.7%	100%
Q4	% lei	−3.5%	−1.9%	−1.8%	0.2%	100%
	% of HHs	96.1%	93.4%	47.1%	46.7%	100%
Q5	% lei	−4.7%	−2.5%	−2.3%	0.0%	100%
	% of HHs	96.1%	93.4%	51.4%	45.2%	100%
All HHs	% lei	−3.9%	−2.4%	−1.5%	0.1%	100%
	% of HHs	96.6%	93.6%	54.4%	51.0%	100%

Source: Public/Private Transfers and Social Capital, World Bank, 2003.

TABLE 8C: NET INFORMAL LENDING

Household Type		Mean Value of Transactions	As a Share of Inter-household Transactions by Quintile	As a Share of Total Income Before a Particular Inter-household Transactions
Q1	lei	−169,044	15.2%	−0.6%
	# of HHs	263	19.2%	50.8%
Q2	lei	−142,819	12.9%	−0.3%
	# of HHs	275	20.1%	53.1%
Q3	lei	255,463	−23.0%	0.4%
	# of HHs	260	19.0%	50.2%
Q4	lei	−323,543	29.1%	−0.4%
	# of HHs	276	20.2%	53.3%
Q5	lei	−730,726	65.8%	−0.4%
	# of HHs	294	21.5%	56.8%
All HHs	lei	−222,134	100%	−0.3%
	# of HHs	1368	100%	52.8%

Source: Public/Private Transfers and Social Capital, World Bank, 2003.

TABLE 8D: NET INFORMAL LENDING (OUTFLOWS AND INFLOWS) (IN LEI PERCENTAGES)

	Outflows			Inflows		
Quintile	Loan Amount	As a Share of Inter-household Transaction by Quintile	As a Share of Income before Inter-household Transaction	Loan	As a Share of Inter-household Transaction by Quintile	As a Share of Income before Inter-household Transaction
Q1	925,222	7.1%	3.4%	756,178	6.4%	2.7%
Q2	1,486,873	11.5%	2.8%	1,344,054	11.3%	2.6%
Q3	1,478,861	11.4%	2.1%	1,734,324	14.6%	2.4%
Q4	2,301,255	17.8%	2.6%	1,977,712	16.7%	2.2%
Q5	6,764,799	52.2%	4.0%	6,034,073	50.9%	3.5%
All HHs	2,591,402	100.0%	3.2%	2,369,268	100.0%	2.9%

Source: Public/Private Transfers and Social Capital Survey, World Bank, 2003.

observation about gifts of agricultural produce and pensions received from rural family members (Table A1a and A2b in Appendix A).

Cash payments for minor services rendered to other households are the second most important transactions in terms of mean value per household and the number of transacting households (54 per cent of households participating). Rural households are more active in these transactions (on average 73 versus 46 per cent respectively, Table 8A and 8B, Appendix A). The rural poor perceive themselves as net winners, while all urban and richer rural households see themselves giving up more resources than they receive. Payments as a share of income before inter-household transfers are mildly progressive as well.

Exchanges of goods and services are more widespread in rural areas, where cash transactions seem to come at a premium—67 percent of rural versus 40 percent of urban sub-samples (Table A8a and A8b, Appendix A). These exchanges are highly progressive, with both the rural and the urban poor seeing themselves as net winners from these transactions.

There are more rural poor households participating in inter-household payments and exchanges than urban poor households. This pattern may reflect closer relationships among neighbors in rural areas, exchanges of foodstuffs for consumption, and payments for minor agricultural services (Table A8a and A8b, Appendix A).

Surprisingly, *informal lending* is found to be regressive. More households from the highest income quintile in rural areas borrow informally than those from the lowest quintile (the opposite is true of urban areas). This finding is backed by statements made during focus group sessions indicating that the poor fear indebtedness and prefer to do without rather than borrow:

> I have nobody to help me, my husband works as well, I have to have milk every day. You can borrow money from a neighbor, but it's quite a shame to ask a second time. I can buy from the kiosk on credit, the owner knows me, they don't help everybody, she understands that I don't have money.
>
> —Low income respondent, Galati, urban

> I can barely make ends meet financially. I hardly even have enough money to buy medicine. I have nobody to help me. I don't dare go and buy on credit, I try to face up to the situation according to my possibilities.
>
> —Low income respondent, Galati, urban

> Generally, you do not borrow. It is better to give up things.
>
> —Low income respondent, Alunis, rural

This may be attributed, on the one hand, to the lack of tradition of professional informal lending in post-Socialist countries, and on the other, to traditional reliance on the state for assistance. The poor, particularly the rural poor, lend more than borrow, which may partly be attributed to the desire to stay in informal networks even if such membership comes at a cost.

At the same time, participation in informal lending is fairly high. Half of all poor households participate in informal lending. Taken separately, informal outflows and inflows equal approximately 4 per cent of total income for poor urban households and 3 and 3.1 per cent respectively for rural households (Table A8e and A8f, Appendix A). These values are comparable to the value of MIG-related transfers. As a share of income, negative balance for the year is fairly small (0.6 per cent of total income) and may represent part of a dynamic borrowing and repayment pattern (Table A8f in Appendix A). These appear to be consumption-smoothing, short-term loans leveraged against in-coming MIG or other public transfers that come with predictable periodicity. Therefore, lending appears an important coping strategy for poor households and part of a consumption-smoothing, risk-sharing exercise.

Maps of Inter-household Transfers

To better understand the current paradigm of exchanges among households, we examine its components:

- Channels of exchanges—relationship among transacting households (relative, friend, and other associate).
- Modality of transactions—altruistic vs. reciprocal exchanges.
- Form of transactions—cash vs. in-kind.
- Geography of exchanges—distance of transactions, the same location vs. other urban/rural localities in Romania or abroad.

The frequency and variety of informal transfers are much greater for richer households than for poorer households and the geography of inter-household connections is much more extended.

TABLE 9: AVERAGE NUMBER OF TRANSACTIONS PER HOUSEHOLD, BY RELATIONSHIP

	All Type of Transfers	Relatives	Friends	Neighbors	Somebody Else	Total
From HH	Very poor (0-4 USD)	2.0	0.7	2.4	1.6	6.7
	Poor (4.1-8 USD)	2.3	0.7	2.0	1.7	6.8
	Average (8.1-16 USD)	2.7	1.0	1.6	1.8	7.1
	Rich (16.1+)	3.5	1.4	1.4	2.0	8.2
	Total	**2.6**	**1.0**	**1.8**	**1.8**	**7.2**
To HH	Very poor (0-4 USD)	1.3	0.4	1.4	0.8	3.9
	Poor (4.1-8 USD)	1.5	0.5	1.0	0.9	4.0
	Average (8.1-16 USD)	1.8	0.7	0.9	1.0	4.3
	Rich (16.1+)	2.3	0.9	0.7	1.3	5.2
	Total	**1.7**	**0.6**	**1.0**	**1.0**	**4.3**

Source: Public/Private Transfers and Social Capital, World Bank, 2003.

Richer households operating in the cash economy carry out more informal transactions in cash. Poorer households conduct more exchanges in goods and services.

Channels and Forms of Informal Transactions—Prohibitive Cost of Friendship

Channels and forms of informal transfers differ dramatically between high income and low income households. Poor households transact primarily with their neighbors, people likely to be in a similar situation, or with providers of odd jobs. These exchanges are predominantly reciprocal, rather than altruistic. The richer households can "afford friendship" with more informal transactions carried out between friends, and more transactions defined as gifts. (Table 9, Figure 1a and 1b).

Households from the poorest income group (from $0–$4 in ppp terms per equivalent adult) transact much less with relatives, both in terms of frequency of exchanges and in total volume of

FIGURE 1A: AVERAGE NUMBER OF TRANSACTION CASES FOR ALL INTERHOUSEHOLD TRANSFERS BY TYPE OF RELATIONSHIP (FROM HH)

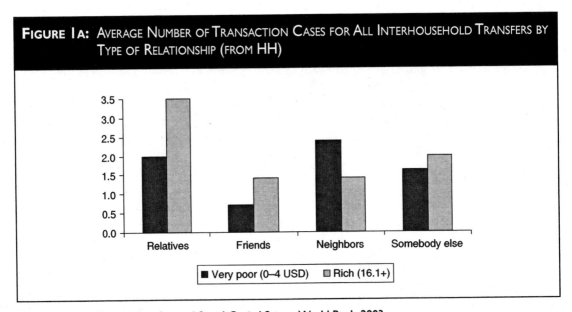

Source: Public/Private Transfers and Social Capital Survey, World Bank, 2003.

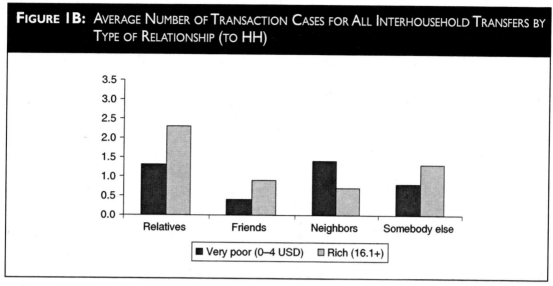

FIGURE 1B: AVERAGE NUMBER OF TRANSACTION CASES FOR ALL INTERHOUSEHOLD TRANSFERS BY TYPE OF RELATIONSHIP (TO HH)

Source: Public/Private Transfers and Social Capital Survey, World Bank, 2003.

transactions, than richer households (Table 10). Poor households average two giving transactions with relatives per year as opposed to an average of 3.5 giving transactions for high income households. The same pattern is observed for receiving transactions—the poor receive an average of 1.3 gifts per year from relatives compared to an average of 2.3 gifts from relatives to high income households. Exchanges with friends are twice as numerous for high-income households than for the poor.

The most likely partner in informal exchanges for the poor are their neighbors. The poor record 40 per cent more giving transactions with neighbors than the high income households and twice as many receiving transactions. Another likely partner for the poor is an associate, which can be explained by the fact that the dominant transaction for the poor is through exchange, rather than altruistic gift giving, as is the case for richer households (Table 10).

> To go and ask from the rich . . . no, we don't do that. We go to the poor. When you are poor, you only go to those who are poor, when you are rich, you go to those who are rich. For if you were to go and ask for help from the rich, they will only laugh at you.
>
> — Low income respondents, Nereju, rural

The Roma poor report isolation within their neighborhoods:

> . . . There are a few (Roma) families round here, on the street that goes up . . . We are like isolated mountains, I swear. We have no water, no roads, we have young children . . . The neighbors won't let us get water from their wells.
>
> —Roma focus group, Aluniş

. . . and high levels of mutual assistance among poor Roma:

> The people in the ghetto help each other. We all rush to help each other. The kids do the same. We don't go to everyone. We know some people. In the end, it is the poor that help each other.
>
> —Roma focus group, Focşani

The poor are much less involved in altruistic exchanges than high income households, but are more involved in gift giving with others (neighbors, other associates)—people in their immediate environment.

TABLE 10: THE STRUCTURE OF INTER-HOUSEHOLD TRANSACTIONS, BY TYPE OF TRANSACTIONS (% OF TOTAL TRANSACTIONS)

Gift or Donations	Relatives		Friends		Neighbors		Somebody Else		Total	
Household Eeconomic Status	From HH	To HH	From HH	To HH	From HH	To HH	From HH	To HH	From HH	To HH
Very poor (0–4 USD)	37%	53%	8%	7%	28%	27%	28%	13%	100%	100%
Poor (4,1–8 USD)	39%	62%	9%	11%	25%	17%	27%	11%	100%	100%
Average (8,1–16 USD)	42%	62%	12%	14%	20%	14%	27%	10%	100%	100%
High Income (16,1+)	47%	61%	15%	18%	15%	11%	25%	11%	100%	100%
Total	**42%**	**60%**	**12%**	**15%**	**20%**	**15%**	**26%**	**10%**	**100%**	**100%**

Loan, Exchange or Payment	Relatives		Friends		Neighbors		Somebody Else		Total	
Household Economic Status	From HH	To HH	From HH	To HH	From HH	To HH	From HH	To HH	From HH	To HH
Very poor (0–4 USD)	25%	24%	11%	10%	45%	39%	20%	28%	100%	100%
Poor (4,1–8 USD)	29%	17%	11%	13%	40%	36%	20%	33%	100%	100%
Average (8,1–16 USD)	27%	19%	20%	16%	31%	27%	21%	38%	100%	100%
High Income (16,1+)	27%	18%	25%	17%	27%	19%	22%	44%	100%	100%
Total	**28%**	**16%**	**17%**	**15%**	**34%**	**31%**	**20%**	**37%**	**100%**	**100%**

Source: Public/Private Transfers and Social Capital Survey, World Bank, 2003.

Th e poor testify to isolation from old friends and to inability to sustain old contacts:

> Relationships have, yes, cooled off among people, because of the differences between . . . how should I phrase this, differences in financial means between people. We had some friends who started their own business . . . now they are doing a lot better than we are, and the relationships between us have cooled off, because you feel at some point that you cannot 'float' at the same level with them, and then you try to contact them less often. They see life differently, it is easier for them to make ends meet . . . that's why we cooled it off.
>
> —Average income respondent, Breaza, urban

> Today's poor are in such terrible shape. (. . .) Because those who are poor today were our friends from yesterday, they are the ones who lived next door to us. They are also their (our former neighbors') children. And these are all relatively educated people. (. . .) They are faced with terribly embarrassing and humiliating circumstances. They cannot pay their bills. (. . .) Some find understanding (from people, institutions), others do not.
>
> —Average income respondents, Focsani, urban

> If you had money you would be everybody's friend, because then you could help everybody. But if I don't have money I cannot even step outside my house. I had friends and I helped them. But now, when they see that I can't work and I can't earn money they don't want to know about it, they don't want to hear anything or see anything. . . . I cannot go and borrow money from a former colleague, whom I used to help before . . . he won't help me, he will say that he is unable to help me, that he can't give me anything.
>
> —Average income residents, Alunis, rural

The rural poor testify to the breakdown of traditional ties of cooperation and traditions of assistance to the poor within communities:

> During Communism people helped each other more. When something happened to Mr. Ion, everyone would jump to his help. Now if something were to happen to him, everyone says, 'Let him manage himself'.
>
> —Focus Group average residents Nereju, rural

Parents and Children

There are more exchanges between parents and children for households in the higher income group than in poor households. There may be three reasons for this pattern. First, higher income people can afford more altruistic exchanges. Second, there are more multigenerational households in poorer income groups. Third, deep poverty is often associated with social rifts and strain of familial ties (Table 11).

As a coping mechanism, poor parents report supporting their adult children from pensions and revenue from agricultural plot production, while children report assisting parents with seasonal agricultural activities:

> My father takes care of me instead of me taking care of him. As soon as he receives his pension, he turns around and lends me money.
>
> —Low income respondent, Breaza, urban

> He [son] comes home on Saturdays, every other week. In the fall, he comes to help harvest potatoes. And I am forced to slaughter a pig every year, because with only one public teacher's salary, you know how these salaries are (. . .).
>
> —Average income respondent, Alunis, rural

Cash at a Premium

The poorer households carry out a higher share of transactions in services and in-kind. Poor households conduct one third of their transactions in cash compared to about half of transactions

TABLE 11: THE AVERAGE NUMBER OF EXCHANGES PER HOUSEHOLD AMONG RELATIVES

All Types of Transfers Household Type	# of HH	Parents		Children		Brother/Sister		Other Relatives	
		From HH	To HH	From HH	To HH	From HH	To HH	From HH	To HH
very poor (0–4)	368 hh	0.5	0.4	0.3	0.2	0.3	0.2	1	0.5
poor (4.1-8)	727 hh	0.4	0.3	0.4	0.4	0.4	0.3	1.1	0.5
average (8.1-16)	983 hh	0.6	0.4	0.5	0.5	0.4	0.3	1.2	0.6
high income (16.1+)	514 hh	0.9	0.7	0.5	0.6	0.6	0.4	1.5	0.7
Total	**2592 hh**	**0.6**	**0.4**	**0.4**	**0.5**	**0.4**	**0.3**	**1.2**	**0.6**

Source: Public/Private Transfers and Social Capital Survey, World Bank, 2003.

for the high-income groups. The poor households also give and receive more services than do high income households (Table 12, Figure 2a and 2b).

It is more difficult for poorer households to participate in cash transactions, as cash transactions require participation in a monetized economy. The increased share of cash transactions is perceived by the poor, particularly the rural poor, as a breakdown of traditions of trust and reciprocity:

> Now everybody is asking for money and it's not like it use to be. In the past you would bring two jars and two bottles for the school fund and it was enough. Now you have to pay hundreds of thousands of lei. I don't have any children of my own who are in school, but I know it is very difficult. My granddaughter is in school . . . My daughter is unemployed, and she is struggling to keep her children in school.
>
> —Female, low income respondents, Galati, urban

> In the past, this is how things would happen. People had their animals, and they would go to their relatives and say, 'Brother-in-law, let me come and help you . . .' He did not want any money for the help offered . . . Or one would offer a free liter of milk, but now if you don't pay, no one gives you any milk! Back then, for example, my cow calved and so she had a lot of milk. Let's say that

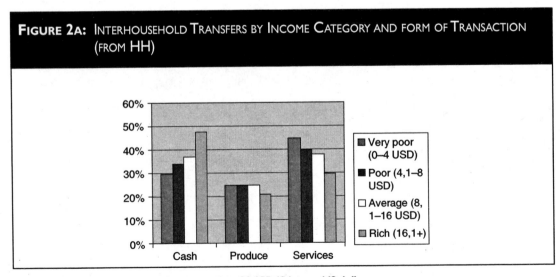

FIGURE 2A: INTERHOUSEHOLD TRANSFERS BY INCOME CATEGORY AND FORM OF TRANSACTION (FROM HH)

Note: In 2002, the average exchange rate was 33,055.40 lei per US dollar.

Source: Public/Private Transfers and Social Capital Survey, World Bank, 2003.

FIGURE 2B: INTERHOUSEHOLD TRANSFERS BY INCOME CATEGORY AND FORM OF TRANSACTION (TO HH)

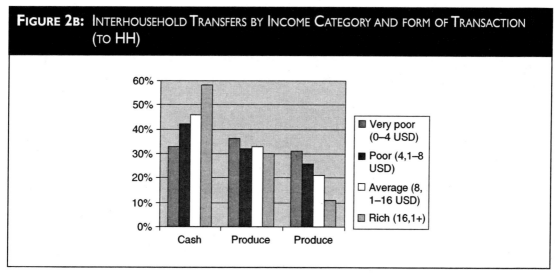

Source: Public/Private Transfers and Social Capital Survey, World Bank, 2003.

would give birth, with calved was gestating also. Well, until your cow would give birth, I would give you milk for free for as long as you needed, and then, later you would give me milk when I had no milk of my own. Now you have to pay for everything upfront. This willingness to help others has eroded . . . this love for other human beings is . . . well, it is no longer as it used to be.

—Male, low income respondent, Alunis, rural

The poor in urban areas report a high monetization of exchanges, even at a very basic level of assistance among neighbors:

One of my neighbors, who lives in this apartment building, helped me move my bed and I gave her 25,000 lei [US$0.75]. She also helps me sometimes, because she has a gas stove and she lets me cook my food on it. I don't have a gas stove, or a gas heating unit, I don't have anything, not even electricity. [. . .] This neighbor also cooks for me sometimes, because my legs hurt and I cannot climb the stairs up to her apartment. She cooks for me, and I give her money out of my pension, and so she helps me.

—Female pensioner, low income respondent, Galati, urban

TABLE 12: INTER-HOUSEHOLD TRANSFERS DEPENDING ON THE HOUSEHOLD ECONOMIC STATUS AND THE FORM OF TRANSACTION (CASH, PRODUCE, SERVICE)

	Household Type	Cash	Produce	Services	Total
From HH	Very poor (0-4 USD)	30%	25%	45%	100%
	Poor (4,1-8 USD)	34%	25%	40%	100%
	Average (8,1-16 USD)	37%	25%	38%	100%
	High income (16,1+)	48%	21%	30%	100%
	Total	**41%**	**24%**	**35%**	**100%**
To HH	Very poor (0-4 USD)	33%	36%	31%	100%
	Poor (4,1-8 USD)	42%	32%	26%	100%
	Average (8,1-16 USD)	46%	33%	21%	100%
	High income (16,1+)	58%	30%	11%	100%
	Total	**51%**	**32%**	**17%**	**100%**

Source: Public/Private Transfers and Social Capital Survey, World Bank, 2003.

TABLE 13: THE STRUCTURE OF INTER-HOUSEHOLD TRANSACTIONS DEPENDING ON THE HOUSEHOLD

All Types of Transfers	Same Locality		Another Village		Another City		Abroad		Total	
Household Economic Status	From HH	To HH	From HH	To HH	From HH	To HH	From HH	To HH	From HH	To HH
Very poor (0-4 USD)	82%	83%	14%	8%	4%	8%	0%	1%	100%	100%
Poor (4,1-8 USD)	78%	78%	14%	10%	8%	11%	0%	1%	100%	100%
Average (8,1-16 USD)	77%	77%	14%	11%	9%	10%	0%	2%	100%	100%
High income (16,1+)	70%	70%	16%	12%	14%	14%	0%	4%	100%	100%
Total	**76%**	**77%**	**15%**	**11%**	**9%**	**11%**	**0%**	**2%**	**100%**	**100%**

Source: Public/Private Transfers and Social Capital Survey, World Bank, 2003.

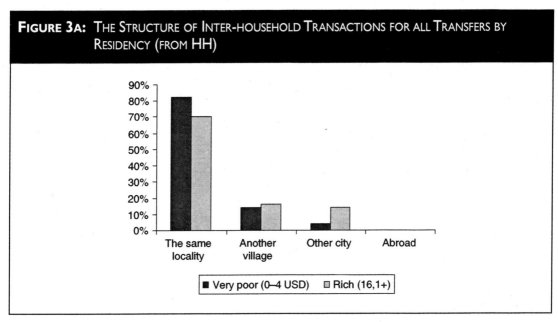

FIGURE 3A: THE STRUCTURE OF INTER-HOUSEHOLD TRANSACTIONS FOR ALL TRANSFERS BY RESIDENCY (FROM HH)

Source: Public/Private Transfers and Social Capital Survey, World Bank, 2003.

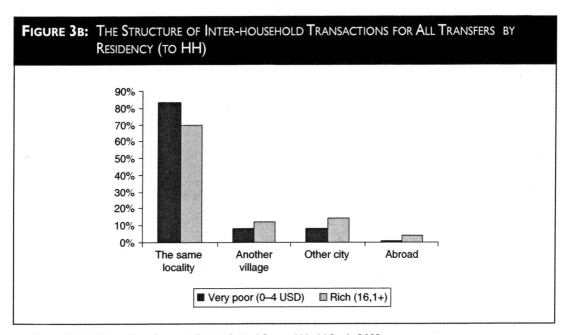

FIGURE 3B: THE STRUCTURE OF INTER-HOUSEHOLD TRANSACTIONS FOR ALL TRANSFERS BY RESIDENCY (TO HH)

Source: Public/Private Transfers and Social Capital Survey, World Bank, 2003.

Geography of Transactions—Distance at a Premium

The difference in the patterns of informal transactions between urban and rural households is also substantial. Populations of large urban settlements (exceeding 100,000 inhabitants), of smaller urban settlements (population below 100,000), and of large rural settlements (more than 5,000 inhabitants) receive a high share of informal flows from abroad in the form of remittances.

The poor, particularly the rural poor, are more confined to transactions in the same localities and have little access to remittances from abroad (Table 13, Figure 3a and 3b).

Conclusion

To conclude, by using an expanded and a more detailed battery of questions than is customary for this kind of inquiry, we find informal transactions to be widespread across all population strata and quintiles (97 per cent of participating households). Informal inflows are an important source of income for poor households, constituting almost 18 per cent of a total household income. A startling finding is that informal transactions are income neutral and, unlike findings in literature on inter-household transfers in both developing and developed countries, do not serve as means-tested flows, an outcome that here is partially attributed to the severance of weak ties and post-socialist dislocation. However, the study also finds that strong familial ties are weaker for the poorer than for the richer quintile as well, as the poor repot giving and receiving significantly fewer gifts from their friends and relatives than does the richest quintile.

While summarily informal transactions are income neutral, individually gift giving and payment for other services are found to be mildly progressive and in-kind exchanges of gifts and services are highly progressive. Surprisingly, informal lending is regressive, attributable to the lack of tradition of usury and other forms of informal lending under socialism, dependence on the state, and apprehension of indebtedness expressed by the poor during the focus group sessions.

Mapping out informal transactions qualitatively, we note that the poor operate in a different paradigm of informality. Informal transactions of the poor are primarily in kind with neighbors, likely to be equally poor, and explicitly reciprocate. Distance, cash, friendship and interactions with relatives come at a premium as they involve additional resources in the case of distance, participating in market transactions (or receiving cash benefits) in the case of cash, and the ability to maintain altruistic gift giving and often costly communications channels in the case of friendship and contacts with relatives. Poverty in Romania leads to greater isolation and substantively different modality of social interactions.

CHAPTER 4

WHO PARTICIPATES IN INFORMAL TRANSACTIONS?

In this section welfare and social capital characteristics of households are examined in relation to the propensity of a household to be a net donor versus a net recipient of flows, or to abstain/be excluded from participating in informal transactions. The relationship between inter-household transactions and social assistance transfers (the MIG program) is examined as well.

Net donors dominate the sample: nearly 60 per cent of respondents perceive themselves to be net donors, and around 37 per cent see themselves as net recipients (see the discussion of this phenomenon above). More rural households are among net donors and significantly less abstain from transacting with other households (Table 14).

Household Welfare

In terms of household welfare, net donors have higher household income, own more assets, and are more satisfied with their current financial status. Net recipients consume more than other categories and find themselves in poorer health. "Others" households not involved in transfers, have the lowest income, own the least assets, and consume less than other households for urban and rural areas respectively. In terms of public assistance, recipients of private transfers are also receiving more Minimum Income Guarantee (MIG) payments than net donors, indicating the potential for a "crowding in" effect. Urban "others" receive the lowest MIG payments, while rural "others" receive the highest MIG-related transfers. The latter may be related to the higher share of multigenerational families among rural "others" than in other groups. The picture is reversed for other social transfers; with urban "others" receiving the highest level of assistance, while rural "others" receive the least non-MIG assistance per household. Such a reversed picture may be connected to the higher level of transparency in rural areas, where the financial status of socially "unconnected" households is more apparent to neighbors as well as to social evaluators for the MIG program (Table 15).

TABLE 14: PARTICIPATION IN INFORMAL TRANSACTIONS

	Number	Percentage
Net Transfer Donors	1545	59.61%
Urban	912	57.72%
Rural	633	62.55%
Net Transfer Recipients	963	37.15%
Urban	605	38.29%
Rural	358	35.38%
Net Transfer Equals Zero (Others)	84	3.24%
Urban	63	3.99%
Rural	21	2.08%
Total	2592	100%
Urban	1580	100%
Rural	1012	100%

Source: Public/Private Transfers and Social Capital Survey, World Bank, 2003.

TABLE 15: WELFARE CHARACTERISTICS

Welfare Characteristics	All Households	Net Donors	Net Recipients	Others
Total Household Income mean in lei	67,200,000	69,500,000	64,300,000	59,700,000
Urban	83,200,000	87,700,000	77,800,000	67,900,000
Rural	42,400,000	43,100,000	41,500,000	35,200,000
MIG Recipients (lei)	822,998	736,669	981,362	595,298
Urban	719,275	622,092	927,441	127,064
Rural	984,936	901,746	1,072,486	2,000,000
Non-MIG Assistance (lei)	1,176,274	873,120	1,342,724	4,843,929
Urban	1,448,751	1,053,869	1,538,205	6,306,103
Rural	750,866	612,704	1,012,372	457,409
Consumption (per adult per day in $)				
(mean)	3.60	3.53	3.71	3.60
Urban	4.29	4.28	4.32	4.23
Rural	2.52	2.46	2.69	1.70
Assets (number of durable goods)	9.20	9.37	8.94	8.83
Urban	10.5	10.75	10.20	9.9
Rural	7.16	7.39	6.82	5.62
Satisfaction with Financial Situation				
(1-10)	4.06	4.16	3.93	3.76
Urban	4.13	4.27	3.94	4.05
Rural	3.95	4	3.93	2.9
Percentage in good health	55.07%	56.33%	52.45%	61.90%
Urban	61.45%	63.56%	58.37%	60.32%
Rural	45.09%	45.87%	42.46%	66.67%

Note: In 2002, the average exchange rate was 33,055.40 lei per US dollar.

Source: Public/Private Transfers and Social Capital Survey, World Bank, 2003.

Household Characteristics

Households not participating in exchanges with other households—"others" in urban areas are older on average, do not live in female-headed households (defined as female respondent and the main breadwinner), and have the highest share of pensioners per household. In rural areas the households not involved in exchanges have more pensioners per household and are most likely to live in a multigenerational household. Net recipients have the highest share of female-headed households and are younger in urban areas. The latter observation is borne by explanations provided in focus groups that older rural parents often transfer resources to urban children in the form of foodstuffs produced on private plots (Table 16).

Social Capital

Different measures of social capital show a pattern for households involved and households not involved in transactions, or "others." "Other" households have a high level of general trust in people, but low levels of specific trust. They trust those living next to them, their neighbors, the least. Urban "other" households feel the least that the poor need assistance, have the least active interactions with neighbors, have fewer close friends, and feel less likely to get assistance in time of need. Most importantly, uninvolved households ("others") do not participate in such collective activities as community projects, local assistance for the needy, or efforts to solve a community problem. However, they are active members of formal private organizations and associations, which is not inconsistent with the self–serving nature of private formal networks discussed above (Table 17).

Inter-household Flows: Multivariate Tests

In this and other studies income tends to be correlated with urban-rural status, household size, and other variables. Multivariate analyses, described in more detail in Appendix B, test the effects of income on inter-household inflows and outflows, controlling for other variables.

TABLE 16: HOUSEHOLD CHARACTERISTICS

HH Characteristics	All Households	Net Donors	Net Recipients	Others
Age of the Subject	52.23	52.12	52.21	54.49
Urban	50.56	51.02	49.47	54.44
Rural	54.83	53.70	56.83	54.62
Share of Female Headed HH	15.93%	13.46%	20.46%	9.52%
Urban	15.32%	14.14%	17.85%	7.94%
Rural	16.90%	12.48%	24.86%	14.29%
Share of HH with Pensioner Present	59.10%	59.09%	58.77%	63.10%
Urban	53.61%	54.93%	51.07%	58.73%
Rural	67.69%	65.07%	71.79%	76.19%
HH size (number of Individuals)	3.03	3.12	2.91	2.9
Urban	1.06	1.07	1.06	1.02
Rural	3.08	3.21	2.84	3.19
Multigenerational	18.09%	18.12%	17.86%	20.24%
Urban	14.75%	15.13%	14.21%	14.29%
Rural	23.32%	22.43%	24.02%	38.10%

Source: Public/Private Transfers and Social Capital Survey, World Bank, 2003.

Table 17: Social Capital

Social Capital	All Households	Net Donors	Net Recipients	Others
Trusting other people	37.03%	36.78%	37.01%	41.67%
Urban	36.08%	36.26%	35.27%	41.27%
Rural	38.52%	37.54%	40.00%	42.86%
Trusting neighbors	57.98%	58.54%	57.39%	54.32%
Urban	60.51%	61.29%	59.72%	56.67%
Rural	54.11%	54.65%	53.54%	47.62%
Need to help the poor	65.13%	65.42%	65.30%	57.69%
Urban	64.65%	64.71%	65.54%	55.17%
Rural	65.85%	66.39%	64.91%	65.00%
Relationship with neighbors	0.209	0.211	0.210	0.156
Urban	0.193	0.196	0.192	0.163
Rural	0.233	0.233	0.239	0.133
Number of close friends	8.208	8.396	8.086	6.159
Urban	7.669	8.075	7.293	5.452
Rural	9.067	8.863	9.479	8.35
Ability to get help when in need	1.838	1.864	1.853	1.19
Urban	2.062	2.13	2.031	1.365
Rural	1.488	1.48	1.55	0.667
Collective Action and Cooperation	0.0013	0.0047	0.0006	−0.0534
Urban	0.0079	0.0103	0.0117	−0.0625
Rural	−0.0090	−0.0034	−0.0181	−0.0261
Groups and Networks				
Number of memberships in				
different org.	1.076	1.0460	1.0620	1.7857
Urban	1.2076	1.1732	1.1802	1.9683
Rural	0.8706	0.8626	0.8631	1.2381

Source: Public/Private Transfers and Social Capital Survey, World Bank, 2003.

In these tests, MIG income is positively but weakly related to gross inflows. Other social assistance income is strongly associated with higher inflows. Net inflows—inflows minus outflows—are unrelated to MIG assistance. These results are consistent with the possibility that public assistance does not "crowd out" private transfers: "crowd out" would be indicated by an inverse relationship between MIG and inter-household inflows. However, the measured relationships could capture both a (negative) "crowd out" effect and a (positive) effect of otherwise unobserved characteristics associated with need. Only by controlling fully for a household's need for private assistance, with variables other than MIG assistance, could we confidently attribute the MIG coefficient to the effects of "crowd out" or absence of "crowd out".

On balance, inter-household transactions are neither progressive nor regressive: holding other factors constant, income is unrelated to net inflows. Assets, however, are significantly related to lower net inflows; by this measure, inter-household transactions have progressive effects. Inflows and outflows are both higher for land owners, and lower for home owners, but neither variable is related to net inflows.

Outflows, but not inflows, are higher for rural than for urban households, controlling for other factors. Net inflows are more negative for rural than for urban households. Inflows and net inflows (but not outflows) increase with age up to about age 68, and then decline as age increases further. Inflows (but not net inflows, or outflows) are lower in households with more adults, and higher in households with more children.

Inter-household Flows and MIG Assistance

Inter-household transactions could potentially affect the level of MIG social assistance received. Households receiving gifts, loans or other inflows might be less likely to apply for MIG than other equally poor households that benefit less from inter-household transactions. Those that apply might be less likely to qualify, or may qualify for more modest benefits if these transactions make them better off—for example, if they use gifts to purchase assets that count against MIG eligibility. Table 15 shows that rural households not involved in inter-household exchanges receive far higher levels of MIG assistance than those that are, suggesting the possibility of "crowd out" of public assistance by private informal assistance. Table 15 also shows, however, evidence of "crowd in" among urban households: those involved in inter-household transactions actually receive much higher MIG and other assistance than other households. Because urban-rural differences are related to income levels and to the volume of inter-household transactions, a fuller investigation of these relationships requires multivariate analysis, described more fully in Appendix B.

These multivariate tests show no evidence to suggest that the benefits to the poor from inter-household transactions are offset by accompanying reductions in their public assistance benefits. These tests are not conclusive, however, as they cannot fully control for factors that may affect either eligibility for MIG or gifts and informal loans received. There is some reassuring evidence that MIG works as planned: households receive more assistance if they have more children, lower incomes, fewer luxury assets, or fewer assets with income-producing potential.

More unsettling are several findings that suggest benefits are affected by other factors unrelated to need, weakening the pro-poor redistributive impact of MIG. Benefits are lower—controlling for income and other variables—in localities that raise fewer revenues locally, and have mayors from the PSD (the ruling Social Democratic Party) or who have been in office longer, suggesting that political influence might affect allocations independently of need. Benefits are also lower in municipalities with fewer Roma.

In the chapter that follows we examine whether the level and forms of social capital in a locality as a collective resource affects the accountability of local government, the level of corruption, the performance of local officials, and the level of trust in those officials. We also examine the effect of social capital on policy execution; here social service delivery, effectiveness of local administration, and satisfaction with government performance.

CHAPTER 5

SOCIAL CAPITAL, LOCAL GOVERNANCE, AND EMPOWERMENT OF THE POOR

The analysis captures positive effects of measures of community activism and social cohesion on the performance of local government and, alternatively, negative effects of ethnic fractionalization. Importantly, high social capital in a locality is related to higher trust in local administration, specifically, the mayor.

Social Capital and Access to Resources—The Case of Triple Exclusion?

There are multiple and contrasting aspects of "social capital" that can help make government more responsive to citizens' demands at the local and national level. There is certainly no consistent pattern by which the poor are disadvantaged relative to the rich on all of these dimensions of social capital. However, on balance, the evidence from this survey suggests that poorer and rural households may suffer "triple exclusion." Not only do formal and informal market and inter-household activities favor rich and urban households, they also appear to have a more effective voice with respect to government services.

Wealthier (Table 18) and urban (Table 19) households tend to belong to more associations. Trust in "most people" differs little across quintiles, and is slightly higher among rural than urban households. Wealthier individuals tend to have more trust in people in their own villages or neighborhoods. Rural people do as well, no doubt because fewer of them are strangers.

Surprisingly, poorer people have somewhat higher trust in local and central government officials, perhaps because the standards for what constitutes good governance tend to rise with education. The large gap between urban and rural households in trust in local officials is unsurprising, because governments in smaller localities are "closer to the people" and it is easier to satisfy smaller, more homogeneous constituencies. More surprising, however, is the nearly-as-large gap in trust in the central government between urban and rural households.

An index of cooperation with neighbors (e.g. in solving common problems) differs little across quintiles, but is higher for rural than for urban households. Similarly, rural people report having more close friends than urban residents. Across quintiles, the rich report having the most close friends. Not

TABLE 18: SOCIAL CAPITAL BY QUINTILE

	Quintiles				
	1	2	3	4	5
Number of associational memberships	0.71	0.99	1.04	1.3	1.34
% who trust ...					
"Most people"	37.1	37.1	36.3	35.2	39.4
People in village/neighborhood	35.7	34.7	38.8	37	40.5
Local government officials	24.2	22.1	23.2	17	18.9
Central government officials	23.7	21.7	19.8	18.4	17.5
Cooperation with neighbors (0–1)	0.21	0.21	0.2	0.21	0.22
Number of close friends	8.2	7.9	7.2	8.7	9.1
No. of people could borrow cash from	2.1	2.9	2.9	3.4	4.9
Max. amount could borrow (million lei)	18	56	27	40	179
Know someone who could help solve ...					
Health problem	34.9	51.5	53.2	61.2	75
Legal problem	14.5	25.8	27.1	36.5	51.5
Administrative problem	25.1	31.6	30.5	34.3	45.5
Problem with police	15.9	23.9	23.8	30.5	39.6
Problem at bank	10.9	16.1	15.7	25.6	35.8
Problem getting a job	8.9	14.5	18.2	21.2	29.1
Offer "gifts" to solve City Hall problem	11.3	5.1	8.1	9.4	12.5
Satisfied with way treated?	65.3	74.4	69.4	72.3	73.6
Contact local officials on public issue	8.4	6.6	8.7	12.7	15.7
Contact nat'l officials on public issue	0.8	0.2	1.4	3.1	5.3
Civic activism index	−0.08	−0.07	0.01	0.02	0.12
Vote in local elections	93.4	93.6	92.5	92.3	92.1
Vote in national elections	93.4	93.4	91.7	92.3	92.8
Response to community problem					
Do nothing	25.9	22.3	17.0	17.8	17.2
File complaint with authorities	11.2	9.3	8.9	10.2	8.1
Try to solve it alone	14.6	15.0	17.0	16.0	15.9
Try to solve it together with others	40.5	50.4	53.4	52.7	56.5

Source: Public/Private Transfers and Social Capital Survey, World Bank, 2003.

surprisingly, wealthier and urban households report having a larger number of people from which they could borrow 3 or 4 million lei [US$90-121]. In response to a question about the maximum amount of money they could borrow from all sources, wealthy and urban households report far higher amounts. The amount for the top quintile is 10 times that of the lowest quintile (Table 18, Table 19).

The rich are better "connected" than the poor. For each of the six types of problems described, the rich were far more likely than the poor to indicate that they knew someone who could help them solve the problem. Urban-rural differences were less dramatic, but mostly favor urban residents, particularly on contacts who can solve legal problems (Table 18, Table 19).[9]

9. Multivariate tests show that the number of connections who can help solve problems increases with income, education, church membership, and cooperation with neighbors, and decreases with age.

TABLE 19: SOCIAL CAPITAL BY URBAN/RURAL

	Rural	Urban
Number of Associational Memberships	0.87	1.21
% who trust ...		
"Most people"	38.5	36.1
People in village/neighborhood	39.1	36.2
Local government officials	32	14.3
Central government officials	27.5	15.8
Cooperation with neighbors (0–1)	0.23	0.19
Number of close friends	9.1	7.7
No. of people could borrow cash from	2.7	3.6
Max. amount could borrow (million lei)	18	56
Know someone who could help solve ...		
Health problem	46.6	60.6
Legal problem	19.4	38.5
Administrative problem	34.9	32.4
Problem with police	22.5	29.4
Problem at bank	14.3	24.9
Problem getting a job	12.4	22
Offer "gifts" to solve City Hall problem	7.5	10.7
Satisfied with way treated?	73.8	68.4
Contact local officials on public issue	13.7	8.3
Contact nat'l officials on public issue	1.7	2.5
Civic activism index	−0.01	0.01
Vote in local elections	94.9	91.4
Vote in national elections	94.1	91.9
Response to community problem ...		
Do nothing	24.2	18.8
File complaint with authorities	11.7	8.8
Try to solve it alone	14.4	17.5
Try to solve it together with others	49.6	54.8

Source: Public/Public Transfers and Social Capital Survey, World Bank, 2003.

Rich and urban residents are somewhat more likely to report having offered bribes to City Hall employees to get problems solved. Rural residents were more frequently satisfied with the treatment they received from City Hall employees. The poorest quintile reported the lowest satisfaction on average, but there was little difference among the higher four quintiles (Table 18).

The richest quintile contacts local officials regarding broad public issues about twice as often as persons in the bottom two quintiles. Rural residents were much more likely than urban to contact local officials, likely reflecting less severe "free rider" problems where the number of potential beneficiaries is lower. Consistent with this view, rural residents were actually less likely than urban residents to contact national officials regarding public issues, where the scope of collective action problems differs less between urban and rural.

Wealthier citizens score higher on a "civic activism" index, based on reported participation in public meetings, protests, etc. Urban scored slightly higher than rural persons; in smaller communities, person-to-person forms of voice may often act as effective substitutes for some forms of mass participation, such as protests seen in urban areas. Rural residents report slightly higher voting turnout rates in both local and national elections. Surprisingly, the poor report slightly higher voting rates than the wealthy (Table 18, Table 19).

There are substantial differences in how poor and non-poor respondents react to problems that concern other members of the community (Table 18). More than one-fourth in the poorest quintile report that they "do nothing," compared to one-sixth in the wealthiest quintile. The poorest quintile is also most likely to react by filing a complaint with the authorities, while the richest quintile is least likely to react in this manner. People in the middle and upper quintiles more often respond in a pro-active fashion. They are somewhat more likely to report trying to solve the problem alone. The most pro-active and generally most effective solution, however, is to solve community problems together with others. This approach is followed by half or more of respondents in the top four quintiles, led by the richest quintile's 56.5 percent. Only 40.5 percent in the poorest quintile respond in this manner. These poor/rich differences in Table 18 are broadly replicated in rural/urban differences in Table 19.

Social Capital, Local Governance, and Public Assistance

Social capital is not only a resource that gives households access to exchange networks or to well-connected persons who can solve household-specific problems. At the community level, social capital can influence the level of public resources, the way in which they are allocated, and the efficiency with which they are spent. Multivariate analysis of the determinants of MIG assistance indicate that benefits are higher for households residing in localities with high levels of "civic activism," as measured by an index of attending public meetings, participating in protests, participating in election meetings, alerting media to a local problem, and notifying the police or courts about a local problem (Appendix Table B3). Higher civic activism could influence MIG assistance in several ways. First, it may be a factor in obtaining more resources for the locality from county and central governments. Second, to the extent that activism reflects altruism, it could also be associated with greater public support for social assistance programs within the locality. Third, public activism at the local level could be associated with improved accountability of local government, which must consider the possibility citizens will protest in various ways if services are inadequate. To the extent local officials have control over MIG funds and implementation, households residing in communities with greater activism may receive higher MIG assistance. A household's own activism matters, however, only to the degree it contributes to the "public good" of monitoring local government or strengthening the locality's influence over allocation of funds by county and central government. Therefore, a household's own level of activism should be unrelated to MIG assistance, controlling for the mean community level of activism. The household's own level of civic activism turned out to be unrelated to MIG assistance, as expected.

Benefits are also higher in localities with mayors who have been in office longer. There are several possible explanations. More experienced mayors may be more effective in lobbying higher levels of government for transfers to local government budgets. They may administer social assistance programs more effectively. Alternatively, causation may go in the other direction, as mayors who manage to run more successful programs improve their chances of re-election. Benefits are also related to the mayor's political party affiliation. Controlling for other influences, households residing in localities with PSD mayors receive higher MIG benefits. However, it is not clear why having a mayor from the PSD matters, because there is no evidence from the 51 localities included in this study that central and county government use their discretion to favor PSD-governed localities. Transfers from central and county government are no higher in PSD-governed localities, and these transfers are not related to the level of MIG benefits anyway.

Although there are sizeable earmarked transfers from central government for social assistance, the revenue measure most strongly associated with higher MIG benefits is locally-raised revenues per capita. Localities are expected to cover about 20 percent of the cost of MIG from local revenues. There is wide variation in locally raised revenues, however, and many localities—particularly smaller and less wealthy localities which are able to raise fewer revenues locally—do not even come close to covering their 20 percent share of costs. This problem has implications for MIG's progressivity. Heating subsidies, in particular, are higher for urban than for rural households (Appendix Table B3).

Table 20 shows that poor people tend to reside in localities with fewer public resources. Households are sorted by income quintiles. Figures in the table are means, within the quintile, of locality-level characteristics. Households in the poorest quintile live in localities averaging only 470,000 lei [US$14.21] in locally-raised ("own") revenues per capita in 2002. This amount nearly doubles, to 930,000 lei [US$28.13], for the top quintile. Most of this variation is attributable to urban-rural differences. Sorting urban and rural households separately by quintiles, variation in

TABLE 20: LOCAL GOVERNMENT REVENUES PER CAPITA

	Quintiles by Income				
	1	2	3	4	5
Own revenues per capita (millions lei)	0.47	0.65	0.78	0.87	0.93
Urban	0.98	1.03	1	1.04	1.06
Rural	0.26	0.31	0.31	0.33	0.4
Social assistance transfers per capita (millions lei)	0.52	0.49	0.42	0.34	0.3
Urban	0.33	0.27	0.26	0.22	0.23
Rural	0.56	0.66	0.63	0.69	0.64
Total county/central govt. transfers per cap. (millions lei)	2.55	2.99	3.11	3.14	3.22
Urban	3.32	3.34	3.32	3.26	3.32
Rural	2	2.69	2.58	2.69	2.75
Total revenues per capita (millions lei)	3.03	3.64	3.88	4.01	4.15
Urban	4.29	4.37	4.32	4.29	4.38
Rural	2.26	3	2.89	3.02	3.14
Quality of public services index	−0.074	−0.001	−0.011	0.07	0.107
Urban	0.134	0.117	0.098	0.142	0.181
Rural	−0.127	−0.184	−0.162	−0.152	−0.192
Town Hall responsibility only (%)	44	36.3	31.8	28.8	27.3
Urban	24	22.7	23.1	24.1	23.1
Rural	52.1	52.1	49.1	47.9	46.5
% worked on community project	31.4	24.1	20.4	17.1	15
Urban	14.1	12.9	12.1	12.9	12
Rural	36.5	39.2	35.6	35.1	30.1
% gave money for community project	55.3	52.3	50	47.9	47.2
Urban	45.9	45.3	45.6	46.8	45
Rural	59.5	59.2	58.5	59.1	54

Source: Public/Public Transfers and Social Capital Survey, World Bank, 2003.

own revenues per capita is very small. Variation among rural households is somewhat larger, however, with own revenues more than 50 percent larger in the top quintile compared to the bottom quintile.

Transfers from central and county governments that are earmarked for social assistance are more progressive, both overall and among urban households. However, the poorest quintile of rural households tend to live in localities receiving lower social assistance transfers per capita (Table 20).

Moreover, total transfers per capita from county and central government, including those non-earmarked or earmarked for other purposes, are regressive, both overall and among rural households. They are neutral among the urban quintiles (Table 20).

The net effect of these transfers, and of own revenues, is markedly regressive: poorer households are more likely than richer households to live in localities with lower revenues per capita. The difference is small among urban households, but is large among rural households, and there are large urban-rural differences (Table 20).

These effects not only show up in MIG assistance at the household level, but also, and not unexpectedly, appear to influence the quality of local infrastructure and public services. An index was constructed from public officials' responses to questions about the quality of road maintenance, water supply system, public order, and locality cleanliness, relative to "similar localities from your county". Framing the comparison with respect to similar localities could reduce urban-rural differences in the responses substantially. However, a very large gap between urban and rural localities is still observed (Table 20). Although the richest quintile of urban households tends to benefit from better public services, there is otherwise little systematic variation across quintiles. In fact, the richest rural quintile tends to experience the worst public services of all.

Poorer households are systematically more likely to reside in localities where a large percentage of respondents in the household survey think that maintenance of the locality is the sole responsibility of the Town Hall. The poorest two rural quintiles are the most likely to live in such localities (Table 20). However, contributing money or work to community projects is more common in rural than in urban localities, and the quintile in which a household is located makes little difference for the level of such contributions occurring in one's locality (Table 20).

Social Capital and Quality of Public Service Delivery

At the community level, social capital is a collective resource which helps keep public officials accountable, reducing corruption and improving the quality of public services (Putnam 1993; Boix and Posner 1998; Knack 2002). Monitoring government, protesting against incompetence or malfeasance, or expressing one's preferences through voting, writing letters or other means can be viewed as a collective action problem in which a narrowly self-interested citizen may rationally free ride on the efforts of others. Knowledge of politics and public affairs by large numbers of citizens, coupled with their participation through voting and other modes of citizen voice, are crucial for accountable government in two ways. First, it is important for citizens to articulate their preferences so that officials are aware of the public interest, even where government officials are highly competent and motivated purely by concern for this interest. Second, the knowledge and willingness to exercise voice is necessary to potentially check incompetent bureaucrats and the ability of politicians to enrich themselves or the narrow interests that they are allied with. Narrowly self-interested citizens may also find it rational not to vote, attend meetings or protest rallies, or even to acquire information about the performance of public officials.

Social norms and networks that generate voluntary action by citizens help prevent or deter public officials and other narrow interests from exploiting governmental resources and power for their own purposes. Where citizens tend to conform to norms of generalized reciprocity and interpersonal trust is higher, free riding is less frequent. Under these circumstances, governmental performance can be improved by affecting the level and character of political participation, by reducing "rent-seeking," and by enhancing public-interested behaviour. Where trust is higher, voters can more easily overcome the collective action problem in monitoring officials. Where too many citizens "free ride" by being uninformed and unwilling to protest government malfeasance, public officials can more easily indulge in patronage practices and other inefficient policies that serve narrow interests.

In addition to making government more accountable, social capital can potentially improve government performance through a second broad mechanism, by reducing inefficiencies associated with the gridlock that arises from political polarization or change-resistant elites. Where trust and norms of reciprocity are stronger, opposing sides are more likely to agree on the ground rules for debate and resolution of disagreements. Where fewer citizens are motivated by a sense of civic obligation to stay informed and to participate in political life, the extremes on the political spectrum are more likely to dominate the public agenda, and debate becomes more polarized.

Several measures of the quality of public services and of community-level social capital can be aggregated from the household survey data to test these relationships across localities in Romania. The sample for this study was constructed so that, within the constraints of only 2,641 households, it would be as representative at the locality level as possible.

A set of questions inquires about interactions during the last year with various parts of local government: city hall, courts, police, hospitals, and schools. The survey ascertains whether a member of the household tried to solve a problem at each of these institutions. For households responding affirmatively, follow-up questions ask whether the household member offered any "gifts" to employees of these institutions to ensure solution of the problem, and whether the household member was satisfied with the way he or she was treated by the employees. From these questions, two indexes were computed for each locality. First, a corruption index measures the percentage of all interactions with these institutions in each locality in which households indicated that a bribe was offered. This index averages 20.7 percent across localities, ranging from a low of 2.3 percent to a high of 41.8 percent. Second, a "client satisfaction" index measures the percentage of all interactions in which households indicated satisfaction with the way they were treated by employees. This index averaged 76.3 percent, ranging from a low of 56.3 percent to a high of 95.7 percent (Table 20).

Where local government has fewer resources to spend on service delivery, a natural hypothesis is that the quality of services may suffer. Multivariate tests (Appendix B, Table 4) confirm that the client satisfaction index is higher in localities with higher total government expenditures per capita.

Holding expenditures per capita constant, the quality of public services may be higher in smaller localities for two reasons. When government is "closer to the people" it is likely to be better informed about public preferences. In smaller communities, preferences are also likely to be more homogeneous, making it easier to provide a combination of services satisfactory to the majority of households. On the other hand, there may be economies of scale in service provision that make it more difficult to provide quality services for the same level of per capita expenditures in smaller localities. The necessity of traveling relatively long distances in rural areas to visit city hall, courts, hospitals, or schools could reduce satisfaction of some households. On balance it is therefore difficult to predict whether satisfaction will be positively or negatively related to locality size. Results show that the first set of arguments dominates: client satisfaction is negatively and significantly related to size of the locality, as measured by (log of) population.

Mean household income in the locality is unrelated to client satisfaction. Higher-income persons may have higher expectations regarding the quality of services. These expectations could affect the quality of services positively, but they could also raise the threshold for what sort of treatment is considered satisfactory by higher-income survey respondents. The insignificant result for income in this test is consistent with the possibility that these two effects, to the extent they occur at all, roughly offset each other.

The main social capital variable included in these tests is an index of relationships with neighbors. Values of the index are higher in localities where more households report discussing "issues that worry you" with neighbors, trying "to solve common problems together" or "problems that concern the whole community," getting together "to help people in need," and trying "to obtain local authority's support for people in need."

This index of cooperation among residents of the community is positively and significantly related to client satisfaction with local government (Appendix Table B4). An index of civic activism (constructed from items including attending public meetings, participating in protests, participating in election meetings, alerting media to a local problem, and notifying police or courts about a local problem) produces similar results, although with borderline statistical significance.

An alternative approach to measuring social capital uses indicators of potential social polarization, including income inequality and an index of ethnic fractionalization. More ethnically mixed communities have been shown in many studies to be associated with lower levels or quality of public goods and services. These results are typically explained in terms of differing preferences across ethnic groups over issues of public interest (taxation and spending) provision of public services, and distribution of resources among different segments of the community. Public officials might also be less willing to resolve the problems of those from a different ethnic group. If there are relatively few social or economic interactions across ethnic groups there is less opportunity for the dissatisfied citizen to retaliate against the official.

An ethnic fractionalization index was created using 1992 census data for each locality on the population share of Roma, Hungarians, Romanians, and others. Following standard practice, the index was computed as one minus the sum of the squared population shares of each of the four groups. The index varies from a low of 0 for several homogeneous ethnically Romanian localities to a high of .52 for a community with 51 percent Hungarians, 2 percent Roma, and approximately 45 percent Romanians.

As shown in Figure 4, this index is associated with significantly lower levels of client/citizen satisfaction with local government services (also Appendix Table B4). This variable remains (borderline) significant when a second social capital variable—the relations with neighbors index or the civic activism index—is included in the same regression.

Income inequality data by locality were computed from the survey data. Higher inequality (measured by coefficient of variation of total household income) is strongly associated with lower levels of client satisfaction with local government services (Appendix Table B4). In contrast to satisfaction with services, the frequency of offering "gifts" was only weakly related to the social capital and social polarization measures.

Table 21 provides a breakdown of these transactions by type of local government institution. About half of the households overall reported interactions with city hall and with hospitals. Fewer

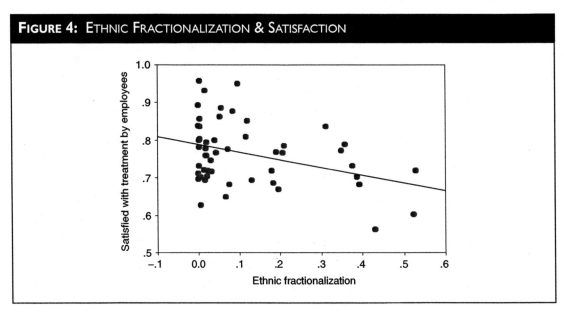

FIGURE 4: ETHNIC FRACTIONALIZATION & SATISFACTION

Source: Public/Private Transfers and Social Capital, World Bank, 2003.

TABLE 21: "SOLVING PROBLEMS" AT LOCAL GOVERNMENT INSTITUTIONS

Institution	% of Households with Interactions	Offered "gifts" (as % of Interactions)	Satisfied with Treatment by Employees		
			as % of All Interactions	as % of Interactions Involving Gifts	as % of Interactions Without Gifts
City Hall	53.2	9.2	70.7	48.0	73.1
Urban	46.4	10.8	68.4	54.4	70.1
Rural	63.9	7.4	73.3	37.6	76.3
Court	14.5	14.9	66.5	41.1	71.6
Urban	16.8	13.4	65.2	40.0	69.9
Rural	11.1	18.6	69.4	42.9	75.9
Police	19.1	10.6	67.1	49.1	69.4
Urban	21.1	11.9	69.7	55.0	71.8
Rural	16.0	8.0	61.7	30.8	64.9
Hospital	47.2	44.5	83.0	72.7	91.3
Urban	48.9	47.4	80.3	70.1	89.7
Rural	44.5	39.7	87.7	78.2	93.8
School	16.4	16.2	86.0	66.2	89.8
Urban	18.1	20.1	84.0	66.7	88.2
Rural	13.7	8.0	90.2	63.6	92.6

Source: Public/Private Transfers and Social Capital, World Bank, 2003.

than 1 in 5 reported interactions with courts, schools, or the police. Interactions with city hall were much more frequent for rural households; interactions with courts, police, hospitals, and schools were all somewhat more frequent for urban households. "Gifts" were offered to government employees in about 45 percent of interactions with hospitals, but were far less frequent in interactions with other institutions.

Satisfaction rates were higher for interactions with hospitals and schools than with other institutions. For each of the five institution types, satisfaction rates were far higher for households which did not report offering gifts. This result does not of course imply that offering gifts is ineffective: gifts may be offered where the prospects of getting one's problem solved are otherwise most bleak. Furthermore, dissatisfaction in part may reflect disgust that it was necessary to offer employees bribes.

Two other, more subjective, measures of the quality of local government were also analyzed: the level of trust in "local government officials," and in the mayor. These indexes are measured on 5-point scales, and aggregated to the local level. Trust in the mayor varies widely across localities, from a low of 1.9 on the 5-point scale to a high of 3.95. The average value is 2.88. Trust in "local government officials" is slightly lower.

Trust in the mayor is higher in smaller localities, consistent with findings described above for client/citizen satisfaction. Public expenditures and mean local income were unrelated to trust. Trust in the mayor is higher where social capital is higher: the relations with neighbors index is positive and significant; so is the civic activism index in results not reported in the table. Trust in the mayor is significantly lower where ethnic fractionalization is higher (Appendix Table B4).[10]

---

10. Findings were similar for trust in local officials, so only results for trust in mayor are reported in Table 4, Appendix B.

Putnam (1993) traces differences in social capital levels between the North and South of Italy to medieval times, when the Normans established a kingdom in Sicily and southern Italy. Americans whose ancestors immigrated—often 100 or more years ago—from areas of Europe with higher levels of social capital retain high levels of social capital today (Rice and Feldman 1997). These findings raise the possibility that the historical experience of different regions in Romania might have had long-lasting impacts on levels of social capital.

The regions dominated by the Ottoman empire well into the 19th century (Wallachia and Moldavia), and by Russia thereafter, differ from those occupied by the Hapsburg empire until 1918 (Transylvania, Banat, and southern Bukovina) in at least several ways that may have potential implications for levels of social capital. First, Protestantism made substantial inroads in Transylvania but not in Wallachia or Moldavia. In comparison with more hierarchically-organized religions (Catholicism, Eastern Orthodoxy, and Islam), Protestantism has been associated with higher levels of interpersonal trust and other measures of social capital in studies using cross-country, cross-state and household-level analyses (Putnam 1993; Fukuyama 1995; La Porta etal. 1997; Putnam 2000; Zak and Knack 2001; Knack 2002). Second, serfdom was abolished by the Hapsburg emperor Joseph II in Transylvania in 1785, while it survived until 1864 in Wallachia and Moldavia. Social capital is generally found to be more prevalent in areas with more egalitarian traditions, as represented by income equality for example (Putnam 1993; Zak and Knack 2001; Knack 2002). Third, the relatively bureaucratized, Weberian public administration of the Hapsburg regions was conducive to greater predictability in interactions among citizens, and between citizens and government. Higher quality public bureaucracy and lower governmental corruption have also been linked to interpersonal trust in cross-country analyses, although causation may run in both directions (Knack and Keefer 1997).

Findings from the Romanian survey data are consistent with these arguments. Table 22 shows differences between the Hapsburg and non-Hapsburg regions of Romania on several measures of social capital. The survey contains numerous questions related to social capital, and differences between the regions are small for the majority of questions. Table 5 shows only those measures for which notable differences emerge; for these, the Hapsburg areas consistently exhibit a higher level of social capital. In the formerly Hapsburg areas, for example, 63 percent agree that most people in the village or neighborhood are trustworthy, compared to only 55 percent in the non-Hapsburg areas. An even larger difference is found for a similar question about people's willingness to help others in need. Residents of the Hapsburg region are more likely to trust the mayor and to report satisfaction with treatment by City Hall employees. Similarly, Hapsburg region respondents were

TABLE 22: HISTORICAL REGIONS AND SOCIAL CAPITAL (IN PERCENT)

	Hapsburg	Non-Hapsburg
Most people in village or neighborhood can be trusted	63.2	54.6
Most people in village or neighborhood are willing to help	57.0	42.8
Solve community problems together with neighbors	30.9	26.2
Attended village or neighborhood meetings or public hearings	31.1	25.6
Only Town Hall should be concerned with maintenance	29.4	34.8
Trust mayor to great extent or very great extent	37.8	32.0
Satisfied with treatment by City Hall employees	76.1	67.7
Offered "gifts" to City Hall employees to solve problem	7.6	10.0
Maximum sample size	987	1647

Source: Public/Private Transfers and Social Capital, World Bank, 2003.

least likely to report offering "gifts," and least likely to say that maintenance of the locality was something that only the Town Hall should be concerned with.[11]

Decentralization and Local Government Efficacy

Decentralized provision of public services is commonly justified on the grounds that local government is better attuned to preferences of its citizens, and that citizens can exercise voice and monitor performance more effectively over local government, because collective action problems among the citizenry are less severe at the local level. Survey evidence in Romania confirms that confidence in local government is higher. About 46 percent of respondents trust central government officials only to a small or very small extent, compared to 42 percent for local government officials, and 37 percent for the mayor. In a Gallup survey conducted in August of 2002, 89 percent of respondents (92 percent of urban and 86 percent of rural) believed that the country was run for the benefit of a few big interests rather than for the benefit of all the people. Only 70 percent (61 percent of rural and 79 percent of urban) believed that their own community was run for the benefit of a few big interests.[12]

However, decentralization can potentially worsen service delivery in localities with few resources and limited administrative capacity, or where responsibilities are not clearly delineated across levels of government. In the survey of 203 local public officials conducted for this study, the most frequent complaint of this sort, for officials of both urban and rural localities, was unfunded mandates from the central government: 73 percent of urban and 46 percent of rural officials cited as a common problem that there were "too many responsibilities assigned to the municipality by central government given present resources" (Table 22). Surprisingly, analysis shows that the frequency of this complaint is unrelated to average incomes, locally-raised revenues, or transfers from central government. Community size and mayor's party are the key determinants of whether local officials perceive unfunded mandates, unclear division of responsibilities, interference from national authorities, and weak local capacity as problems (Table 22). Only concerning "interference from county authorities" do rural officials complain more than urban officials. Officials from localities with non-PSD mayors cite each of the nine problems listed in Table 22 more frequently.

Interestingly, analysis of local government revenue data for the 51 localities represented in these surveys does not support the common view that central government transfers are more generous to localities with PSD mayors. However, a more thorough study of this issue would require analyzing all local governments in the country.

Other survey questions indicate that officials in localities without mayors from the PSD believe their interests are neglected by county and national authorities (Table 23). For example, 41 percent of officials in non-PSD localities, but only 17 percent in localities with PSD mayors, believe the county administration pays less attention to their locality than to other localities in the county. A large percentage of officials from PSD and non-PSD localities believe personal relationships influence funds allocation to local government. Concerning funds from central government, substantially more officials from localities without PSD mayors believe personal relationships are important.

There are no consistent differences in these responses between urban and rural officials. For example, rural are more likely than urban officials to indicate that local elected officials are often consulted by county authorities, but the reverse is true for consultations with national authorities (Table 23).

---

11. When this two-way distinction is replaced by a three-way classification of regions, social capital levels are generally found to be somewhat higher in Wallachia than in Moldavia, although these differences are more modest than those between either region and Transylvania. These regional differences remain when controlling for locality size, urban-rural status, ethnic composition and diversity, and income levels.

12. See Sandu etal. (2000) for similar evidence from surveys conducted in 1997–2000.

TABLE 23: PERCEPTIONS OF INTER-GOVERNMENTAL RELATIONS BY LOCAL OFFICIALS (PERCENT PERCEIVING PROBLEM AS BEING FREQUENT)

	Urban	Rural	PSD	Non-PSD
Too many responsibilities given resources	73.0	46.3	51.2	76.5
Restrictive rules imposed by central government	57.8	30.5	38.3	56.5
Unclear division of responsibility	22.8	13.3	14.8	23.9
Interference from county authorities	16.0	22.7	17.3	22.9
Interference from central authorities	21.2	8.3	10.3	37.1
Too little discretion in revenue-raising	32.0	23.7	22.6	32.9
Too little discretion in expenditure decisions	30.3	22.9	23.2	32.9
Too little authority in development policy	23.5	20.6	16.0	32.9
Insufficient capacity to implement local programs	55.6	39.2	39.4	62.3

Source: Public/Private Transfers and Social Capital, World Bank, 2003.

TABLE 24: PERCEPTIONS OF LOCAL GOVERNMENT INFLUENCE WITH COUNTY OR CENTRAL GOVERNMENT (PERCENT WHO AGREE WITH STATEMENT)

	Urban	Rural	PSD	Non-PSD
County administration pays less attention to your locality than others	22.8	27.8	16.9	41.2
National administration pays less attention to your commune than others	33.0	30.3	23.3	47.0
Funds allocation from county are often based on personal relationships	41.0	45.9	43.9	42.3
Funds allocation from central government are often based on personal relationships	39.1	36.7	35.6	42.3
Local elected officials are frequently consulted by county authorities	78.1	89.9	87.1	77.5
Local elected officials are frequently consulted by national authorities	63.8	57.1	65.2	52.1

Source: Public/Private Transfers and Social Capital, World Bank, 2003.

Given the perceived importance of networks and personal relationships, one would expect localities with longer-tenured mayors to be more influential. However, the officials' surveys do not support this assertion. Officials in localities with re-elected mayors do not perceive greater influence for their localities. For example, officials in localities with re-elected mayors are somewhat more likely to complain that county and national authorities pay less attention to their localities than to others in the county.

CHAPTER 6

POLICY IMPLICATIONS

- Private formal flows are found to be largely regressive, and private informal flows income neutral. The poor appear to be less likely to benefit from both altruistic inter-household flows and transfers from private formal organizations. These observations make well-targeted public assistance even more vital to the livelihood of the poor.

- Controlling for other variables, MIG payments are lower in rural areas. The rural poor do not seem to be receiving their fair share of MIG payments, even though focus groups indicate that they rely on MIG payments for their livelihood more than urban households. The poor count on these payments both as a single source of cash, and as a means of obtaining informal loans. The MIG scheme for rural areas needs to be revisited in terms of levels of benefits.

- MIG targeting is impaired by variables not related to poverty. Smaller and poorer localities get less MIG assistance for their poor. Localities with mayors that have been elected to office more than once get more MIG assistance. Localities that have more active and socially involved populations get more MIG assistance. These findings should be taken into account by policymakers when adjusting MIG targeting schemes.

- While the end result—the benefit—is highly appreciated by the recipients, *the process* of accessing MIG is found to be faulty. This is due to: 1) corruption, 2) indifference and arbitrariness of local officials, 3) high costs of obtaining and filing documentation, and 4) high transactions costs in terms of time and access to information about MIG benefits both in urban and rural areas. This is particularly true of rural areas, where lower average level of education among the poor makes it more difficult to deal with the paperwork and with the multiple offices that need to be visited to file an application, and, ultimately, to receive the benefit. Also, transportation and filing costs are reported to be high and highly varied depending on the locality. The process of filing documentation and eligibility criteria need to be streamlined to leave less room for local officials to arbitrarily increase the burden of proof to the poor, thus opening the door to more bribes and corruption.

- The poor are less likely to have access to public officials at the time of need. The poor are also found to be less socially active and less likely to defend their rights at the local and national levels. A special outreach program could be designed for public officials to initiate contacts with residents of poor areas to get a better picture of their needs and to provide assistance in a more timely manner.
- Social capital, on balance, was found to positively affect interactions between local administration and the population as well as execution of public programs. Furthermore, a socially active stance is positively related to social assistance, specifically, MIG-related programs. There are no clear recipes for building social capital. The history of interaction between the population and the state importantly also affects trust and collective action. However, public policies that encourage transparent channels of resource distribution and empower the population, particularly the poor, to participate in budgetary decision-making is likely to encourage activism, and to improve targeting of social assistance programs at the community level.
- Controlling for other variables, areas with a higher share of Roma in the population are receiving lower levels of MIG assistance. A separate strategy needs to be developed for reaching the Roma poor.
- Total transfers per capita from county and central government are found to be regressive both overall and among rural households, with the net effect that poorer households are more likely to live in localities with lower revenue than richer households. These finding are compounded by the results that activism levels are lower among the poor. Therefore, for the government to be successful in its anti-poverty campaign, other transfers, not just MIG-related flows, need to be distributed in a less regressive manner.

APPENDIX TABLES

TABLE A1A: NET TOTAL INCOME—URBAN AVERAGE FOR 2002—BY NUMBER OF HOUSEHOLDS (1,540 HOUSEHOLDS)

Household Type		Formal Income (A) (1+2+3)	Formal Earned Income — Salary (1)	Private Business (2)	Net Formal Transfer (3) (a+b+c+d)	Public Social Benefits (a)	Public Social Assistance (b)	Other Transfers from Formal Public Sources (c)	Transfers from Formal Private Sources (d)	Informal Income (B) (f+g+h)	Informal Wages, Small Scale Agricultural Production and Leasing of Land (f)	Gift (g)	Exchange (h)	Other (C)	Total Income (A+B+C)
Q1	lei	29,824,220	12,600,000	1,429,918	15,794,302	11,900,000	1,400,497	2,427,328	66,477	-1,406,833	4,925,305	-6,463,759	131,621	1,940,098	30,357,485
	#HHs	149	64	9	140	124	53	68	4	150	150	141	43	32	150
Q2	lei	47,449,681	29,200,000	1,332,836	16,916,845	13,600,000	898,093	2,137,355	281,397	3,141,203	6,867,668	-3,267,010	-459,455	3,725,823	54,301,595
	#HHs	267	188	13	252	238	78	117	15	268	268	254	47	59	268
Q3	lei	64,011,324	40,800,000	1,281,846	21,929,478	17,300,000	596,689	3,513,056	519,732	4,242,150	6,493,404	-2,187,453	-63,801	3,013,653	71,346,819
	#HHs	324	226	15	283	262	65	143	27	325	325	302	64	64	325
Q4	lei	79,015,241	49,700,000	1,973,259	27,341,982	21,600,000	814,276	4,403,835	523,872	6,820,474	9,567,489	-2,905,522	158,507	4,447,410	90,256,237
	#HHs	389	248	20	345	313	82	189	29	391	391	364	82	102	391
Q5	lei	151,112,114	77,100,000	29,000,000	45,012,114	22,900,000	1,085,470	17,000,000	4,026,644	16,574,422	13,043,888	3,253,891	276,643	8,895,891	176,771,686
	#HHs	404	257	56	346	302	79	227	31	406	406	381	83	108	406
Total	lei	84,480,590	47,800,000	8,776,669	27,903,921	18,700,000	911,793	6,933,801	1,358,327	7,401,479	8,912,685	-1,543,705	32,499	4,945,530	96,873,060
	#HHs	1,533	983	113	1,366	1,239	357	744	106	1542	1542	1,444	319	365	1542
Q1	% lei	98.24%	41.51%	4.71%	52.03%	39.20%	4.61%	8.03%	0.22%	-4.63%	16.29%	-21.29%	0.44%	6.42%	100%
	% HHs	98.68%	42.38%	5.96%	92.72%	82.12%	35.10%	45.03%	2.65%	100.00%	100.00%	94.04%	28.48%	21.19%	100%
Q2	% lei	87.36%	53.76%	2.45%	31.14%	25.04%	1.65%	3.94%	0.52%	5.78%	12.65%	-6.01%	-0.85%	6.86%	100%
	% HHs	99.63%	70.15%	4.85%	94.03%	88.81%	29.10%	43.66%	5.60%	100.00%	100.00%	94.78%	17.54%	22.01%	100%
Q3	% lei	89.82%	57.25%	1.80%	30.77%	24.27%	0.84%	4.92%	0.73%	5.95%	9.10%	-3.07%	-0.09%	4.22%	100%
	% HHs	99.69%	69.54%	4.62%	87.08%	80.62%	20.00%	44.00%	8.31%	100.00%	100.00%	92.92%	19.69%	19.69%	100%
Q4	% lei	87.52%	55.05%	2.19%	30.28%	23.92%	0.90%	4.88%	0.58%	7.85%	10.60%	-3.22%	0.18%	4.93%	100%
	% HHs	99.23%	63.27%	5.10%	88.01%	79.85%	20.92%	48.21%	7.40%	100.00%	100.00%	93.11%	20.92%	26.02%	100%
Q5	% lei	85.58%	43.66%	16.42%	25.49%	12.97%	0.61%	9.62%	2.28%	9.69%	7.38%	1.84%	0.16%	5.03%	100%
	% HHs	99.51%	63.30%	13.79%	85.22%	74.38%	19.46%	55.91%	7.64%	100.00%	100.00%	93.84%	20.44%	26.60%	100%
Total	% lei	87.25%	49.37%	9.06%	28.82%	19.31%	0.94%	7.16%	1.40%	7.64%	9.20%	-1.59%	0.03%	5.11%	100%
	% HHs	99.42%	63.75%	7.33%	88.59%	80.35%	23.15%	48.25%	6.87%	100.00%	100.00%	93.64%	20.69%	23.67%	100%

Formal Income: salary, income through civil convention/ collaboration contract, independent authorized non/agricultural activities, State old age pension, Veteran or disability pension, CAP pension, scholarships, child benefits, other social payments, income from investments, savings, rent on other properties, income from business profit, formal public and private assistance (such as social allowances, emergency relief, etc.) *Formal Transfers*: state old age pension + veteran pension or disability pension + CAP pension + scholarship + child benefits + other social payments + formal public and private assistance (such as social allowances, emergency relief, etc.) *Public Social Benefit*: State old age pension, Veteran or disability pension, CAP pension, scholarships, child benefits; *Public Social Assistance*: social allowances, emergency relief, allowances for the wives of conscripts, subsidies for heating dwellings connected to the public heating system, subsidies for heating by fuel, firewood and/or coal; *Other Transfers from Formal Public Sources*: Formal public assistance from the local council, police, prefect's office, National Government, City Hall, Communal administration agency, and public hospitals and schools; subventions for medical assistance (e.g. surgery); subsidies for agricultural services; subsidized loans for building/ buying a house; *Transfers from Formal Private Sources*: Formal private assistance from associations such as the Village/Neighborhood committee and Parents' committee, and private schools and hospitals + money from sponsors + donations; *Informal Income Total*: daily wages, small scale agricultural production, leasing of land, others, net gift and donations, net exchanges of services, payments; *Earning from Agriculture and informal daily wages*: income from daily work or temporary incomes, income from household agricultural production, yearly self- consumption; *Income from Rent and Leasing of Land*: income for land rented for use, income for land leased to others; *Net exchange*: exchange of similar and different services; *Other informal sources*: payment inflow, money from relatives who work temporarily in another country, other sources.

Source: Public/Private Transfers and Social Capital Survey, World Bank, 2003.

TABLE A1B: NET TOTAL INCOME—RURAL AVERAGE FOR 2002—BY NUMBER OF HOUSEHOLDS (1,540 HOUSEHOLDS)

Household Type		Formal Income (A) (1+2+3)	Formal Earned Income: Salary (1)	Private Business (2)	Net Formal Transfer (3) (a+b+c+d)	Formal Transfer by Category: Public Social Benefits (a)	Public Social Assistance (b)	Other Transfers from Formal Public Sources (c)	Transfers from Formal Private Sources (d)	Informal Income (B) (f+g+h)	Informal Income by Category — Informal Inter-household Transfers: Informal Wages, Small Scale Agricultural Production and Leasing of Land (f)	Gift (g)	Exchange (h)	Other (C)	Total Income (A+B+C)
Q1	lei	15,687,908	4,419,134	544,138	10,724,636	8,797,417	695,518	1,136,713	94,989	4,936,687	8,358,189	-3,304,149	-117,353	2,507,066	23,131,661
	#HHs	333	66	10	323	299	80	152	10	367	364	341	291	183	367
Q2	lei	33,051,958	13,900,000	899,203	18,252,755	15,100,000	855,904	2,207,242	89,609	9,022,758	11,322,093	-2,649,025	349,690	2,715,695	44,790,411
	#HHs	244	93	8	235	226	35	117	18	251	250	238	219	101	251
Q3	lei	48,694,778	22,000,000	1,713,918	24,980,860	19,100,000	1,006,031	3,986,611	888,218	10,887,350	12,944,237	-2,515,597	458,710	4,577,909	64,160,037
	#HHs	191	86	8	185	175	31	97	15	194	192	179	198	69	194
Q4	lei	55,203,579	25,800,000	2,824,778	26,578,801	19,500,000	1,299,127	5,215,944	563,730	17,627,256	18,769,856	-1,153,420	10,820	5,370,812	78,201,647
	#HHs	125	53	6	117	112	22	62	12	126	126	119	150	54	126
Q5	lei	77,321,923	33,300,000	7,299,628	36,722,295	20,800,000	3,718,393	10,800,000	1,403,902	42,799,129	42,200,000	-581,651	1,180,780	22,926,696	143,047,748
	#HHs	109	41	13	102	95	22	62	9	112	112	104	145	38	112
Total	lei	37,299,243	15,600,000	1,839,408	19,859,835	14,800,000	1,186,102	3,437,606	436,127	12,624,382	14,823,169	-2,453,362	254,575	5,457,225	55,380,851
	#HHs	1,002	339	45	962	907	190	490	64	1050	1,044	981	1003	445	1,050
Q1	% lei	67.82%	19.10%	2.35%	46.36%	38.03%	3.01%	4.91%	0.41%	21.34%	36.13%	-14.28%	-0.51%	10.84%	100.00%
	% HHs	90.74%	17.98%	2.72%	88.01%	81.47%	21.80%	41.42%	2.72%	100.00%	99.18%	92.92%	79.29%	49.86%	100.00%
Q2	% lei	73.79%	31.03%	2.01%	40.75%	33.71%	1.91%	4.93%	0.20%	20.14%	25.28%	-5.91%	0.78%	6.06%	100.00%
	% HHs	97.21%	37.05%	3.19%	93.63%	90.04%	13.94%	46.61%	7.17%	100.00%	99.60%	94.82%	87.25%	40.24%	100.00%
Q3	% lei	75.90%	34.29%	2.67%	38.94%	29.77%	1.57%	6.21%	1.38%	16.97%	20.17%	-3.92%	0.71%	7.14%	100.00%
	% HHs	98.45%	44.33%	4.12%	95.36%	90.21%	15.98%	50.00%	7.73%	100.00%	98.97%	92.27%	102.06%	35.57%	100.00%
Q4	% lei	70.59%	32.99%	3.61%	33.99%	24.94%	1.66%	6.67%	0.72%	22.54%	24.00%	-1.47%	0.01%	6.87%	100.00%
	% HHs	99.21%	42.06%	4.76%	92.86%	88.89%	17.46%	49.21%	9.52%	100.00%	100.00%	94.44%	119.05%	42.86%	100.00%
Q5	% lei	54.05%	23.28%	5.10%	25.67%	14.54%	2.60%	7.55%	0.98%	29.92%	29.50%	-0.41%	0.83%	16.03%	100.00%
	% HHs	97.32%	36.61%	11.61%	91.07%	84.82%	19.64%	55.36%	8.04%	100.00%	100.00%	92.86%	129.46%	33.93%	100.00%
Total	% lei	67.35%	28.17%	3.32%	35.86%	26.72%	2.14%	6.21%	0.79%	22.80%	26.77%	-4.43%	0.46%	9.85%	100.00%
	% HHs	95.43%	32.29%	4.29%	91.62%	86.38%	18.10%	46.67%	6.10%	100.00%	99.43%	93.43%	95.52%	42.38%	100.00%

Formal Income: salary, income through civil convention/ collaboration contract, independent authorized non/agricultural activities, State old age pension, Veteran or disability pension, CAP pension, scholarships, child benefits, other social payments, income from investments, savings, rent on other properties, income from business profit, formal public and private assistance (such as social allowances, emergency relief, etc.) *Formal Transfers:* state old age pension + veteran pension or disability pension + CAP pension + scholarship + child benefits + other social payments + formal public and private assistance (such as social allowances, emergency relief, etc.) *Public Social Benefit:* State old age pension, Veteran or disability pension, CAP pension, scholarships, child benefits; *Public Social Assistance:* social allowances, emergency relief, allowances for the wives of conscripts, subsidies for heating dwellings connected to the public heating system, subsidies for heating by fuel, firewood and/or coal; *Other Transfers from Formal Public Sources:* Formal public assistance from the local council, police, prefect's office, National Government, City Hall, Communal administration agency, and public hospitals and schools; subventions for medical assistance (e.g. surgery); subsidies for agricultural services; subsidized ticket for traveling by rail; subsidized loans for building/ buying a house; *Transfers from Formal Private Sources:* Formal private assistance from associations such as the Village/Neighborhood committee and Parents' committee, and private schools and hospitals + money from sponsors + donations; *Informal Income Total:* daily wages, small scale agricultural production, leasing of land, others, net gift and donations, net exchanges of services, payments; *Earning from Agriculture and informal daily wages:* income from daily work or temporary incomes, income from household agricultural production, yearly self- consumption; *Income from Rent and Leasing of Land:* income for land rented for use, income for land leased to others; *Gift:* gift inflow–gift outflow; *Net exchange:* exchange of similar and different services; *Other informal sources:* payment inflow, money from relatives who work temporarily in another country, other sources.

Source: Public/Private Transfers and Social Capital Survey, World Bank, 2003.

TABLE A2A: TRANSFERS FROM PUBLIC SERVICE PROVIDING INSTITUTIONS AND FROM PUBLIC ASSISTANCE PROGRAMS, BY QUINTILE (URBAN, RURAL)

Urban

Variable	Average Amount of Transfers from Public Service Providers	As a Share of the Transfer	As a Share of Income before the Transfer	Average Amount of Transfers from Other Public Programs	As a Share of the Transfer	As a Share of Income before the Transfer
Quintile 1	758,558	5.6%	2.73%	1,668,770	2.9%	6.00%
Quintile 2	750,858	10.0%	1.42%	1,386,497	4.3%	2.63%
Quintile 3	898,450	14.8%	1.32%	2,614,606	10.1%	3.85%
Quintile 4	1,213,785	22.4%	1.42%	3,190,050	13.8%	3.72%
Quintile 5	2,537,384	51.3%	1.60%	14,462,616	68.8%	9.10%
All HHs	1,320,522	100.0%	1.47%	5,613,279	100.0%	6.24%

Rural

Variable	Average Amount of Transfers from Public Service Providers	As a Share of the Transfer	As a Share of Income before the Transfer	Average Amount of Transfers from Other Public Programs	As a Share of the Transfer	As a share of Income before the Transfer
Quintile 1	358,443	21.3%	1.62%	778,270	9.6%	3.52%
Quintile 2	385,270	15.5%	0.91%	1,821,972	15.1%	4.29%
Quintile 3	547,730	16.3%	0.91%	3,438,881	21.2%	5.71%
Quintile 4	881,742	20.4%	1.22%	4,334,202	20.7%	5.98%
Quintile 5	1,629,057	28.2%	1.24%	9,170,943	32.8%	7.00%
All HHs	588,846	100.0%	1.14%	2,848,760	100.0%	5.51%

Source: Public/Private Transfers and Social Capital Survey, World Bank, 2003.

Amount (lei)[11]	1	2	3	4	5	6	7	8	9	10	11	12
TABLE A4A: MONETARY TRANSFERS (OUTFLOWS) TO PRIVATE ORGANIZATIONS												
less than 110,000	483	98	65	11	39	24	14	0	6	2	8	1
between 110–510,000	921	200	156	10	26	26	22	11	14	6	12	2
510,000–1,000,000	149	32	64	6	10	3	13	14	12	6	2	4
between 1,1–1,000,000	77	13	26	29	1	5	10	11	10	12	6	5
over 3,000,000	32	5	5	61	2	13	12	13	6	8	0	2
Total	**1,662**	**348**	**316**	**117**	**78**	**71**	**71**	**49**	**48**	**34**	**28**	**14**

Ranking:
  1. *Church Committee Or Other Forms Of Collective Church Coordination*
  2. *Parents' Committee*
  3. *Trade Union Or Labour Union*
  4. *Agricultural Society With Legal Personality*
  5. *Political Party*
  6. *Other Associations*
  7. *Professional Association*
  8. *Money-Rotating System*
  9. *Artists' / Sports Association*
  10. *Family-Type Agricultural Association*
  11. *NGO Or Civic Group*
  12. *Traders Or Business Association*

Source: Public/Private Transfers and Social Capital Survey, World Bank, 2003.

TABLE A6c: URBAN INTER-HOUSEHOLD TRANSACTIONS OUTFLOWS (IN LEI AND PERCENTAGES)

Quintile	Number of HHs	Inter-household Transaction	Gift	Payment	Exchange	Income before Inter-household Transaction
Q1	150	5,191,064	3,318,928	1,046,765	825,371	32,500,000
Q2	270	6,127,173	4,603,356	1,060,821	462,996	58,000,000
Q3	334	7,364,511	5,375,121	1,505,110	484,280	72,500,000
Q4	334	9,151,397	6,428,573	2,316,658	406,166	91,900,000
Q5	375	20,259,871	14,700,000	4,138,489	1,421,382	176,000,000
All HHs	1,540	10,804,319	7,776,479	2,282,993	744,847	98,400,000
As a Share of Total Inter-household Transactions						
Q1		100.0%	63.9%	20.2%	15.9%	
Q2		100.0%	75.1%	17.3%	7.6%	
Q3		100.0%	73.0%	20.4%	6.6%	
Q4		100.0%	70.2%	25.3%	4.4%	
Q5		100.0%	72.6%	20.4%	7.0%	
All HHs		100.0%	72.0%	21.1%	6.9%	
As a Share of a Particular Inter-household Transaction						
Q1		4.7%	4.2%	4.5%	10.8%	3.2%
Q2		9.9%	10.4%	8.1%	10.9%	10.3%
Q3		14.8%	15.0%	14.3%	14.1%	16.0%
Q4		18.4%	17.9%	22.0%	11.8%	20.3%
Q5		45.7%	46.0%	44.1%	46.5%	43.6%
All HHs		100.0%	100.0%	100.0%	100.0%	100.0%
As a Share of Income before a Particular Inter-household Transaction						
Q1		16.0%	10.2%	3.2%	2.5%	
Q2		10.6%	7.9%	1.8%	0.8%	
Q3		10.2%	7.4%	2.1%	0.7%	
Q4		10.0%	7.0%	2.5%	0.4%	
Q5		11.5%	8.4%	2.4%	0.8%	
All HHs		11.0%	7.9%	2.3%	0.8%	

Source: Public/Private Transfers and Social Capital, World Bank, 2003.

TABLE A6D: URBAN INTER-HOUSEHOLD TRANSACTIONS INFLOWS (IN LEI AND PERCENTAGES)

Quintile	Number of HHs	Inter-household Transaction	Gift	Payment	Exchange	Income before Inter-household Transaction
Q1	150	6,037,941	4,099,457	857,698	1,080,786	32,500,000
Q2	270	4,386,233	3,385,134	555,869	445,230	58,000,000
Q3	334	5,193,232	3,635,868	1,039,321	518,043	72,500,000
Q4	334	4,618,732	3,635,868	242,871	739,993	91,900,000
Q5	375	8,154,787	6,301,342	723,859	1,129,586	176,000,000
All HHs	1,540	7,532,794	6,096,711	658,737	777,346	98,400,000
As a Share of Total Inter-household Transactions						
Q1		100.0%	67.9%	14.2%	17.9%	
Q2		100.0%	77.2%	12.7%	10.2%	
Q3		100.0%	70.0%	20.0%	10.0%	
Q4		100.0%	78.7%	5.3%	16.0%	
Q5		100.0%	77.3%	8.9%	13.9%	
All HHs		100.0%	80.9%	8.7%	10.3%	
As a Share of a Particular Inter-household Transaction						
Q1		7.8%	6.5%	12.7%	13.5%	3.2%
Q2		10.2%	9.7%	14.8%	10.0%	10.3%
Q3		15.0%	12.9%	34.2%	14.5%	16.0%
Q4		13.3%	12.9%	8.0%	20.6%	20.3%
Q5		26.4%	25.2%	26.8%	35.4%	43.6%
All HHs		100.0%	100.0%	100.0%	100.0%	100.0%
As a Share of Income before a Particular Inter-household Transaction						
Q1		18.6%	12.6%	2.6%	3.3%	
Q2		7.6%	5.8%	1.0%	0.8%	
Q3		7.2%	5.0%	1.4%	0.7%	
Q4		5.0%	4.0%	0.3%	0.8%	
Q5		4.6%	3.6%	0.4%	0.6%	
All HHs		7.7%	6.2%	0.7%	0.8%	

Source: Public/Private Transfers and Social Capital Survey, World Bank, 2003.

TABLE A6E: RURAL INTER-HOUSEHOLD TRANSACTIONS OUTFLOWS (IN LEI AND PERCENTAGES)

Quintile	Number of HHs	Inter-household Transaction	Gift	Payment	Exchange	Income before Inter-household Transaction
Q1	368	4,782,012	2,637,468	1,152,715	991,829	25,600,00
Q2	248	8,090,517	4,885,778	2,348,439	856,300	46,300,000
Q3	184	8,234,901	4,827,455	2,652,025	755,421	68,100,000
Q4	143	13,499,388	7,881,469	3,839,498	1,778,421	78,600,000
Q5	107	20,894,645	8,003,396	11,300,000	1,591,249	147,000,000
All HHs	1,050	8,995,086	4,813,263	3,095,222	1,086,601	57,600,000
As a Share of Total Inter-household Transactions						
Q1		100.0%	55.2%	24.1%	20.7%	
Q2		100.0%	60.4%	29.0%	10.6%	
Q3		100.0%	58.6%	32.2%	9.2%	
Q4		100.0%	58.4%	28.4%	13.2%	
Q5		100.0%	38.3%	54.1%	7.6%	
All HHs		100.0%	53.5%	34.4%	12.1%	
As a Share of a Particular Inter-household Transaction						
Q1		18.6%	19.2%	13.1%	32.0%	15.6%
Q2		21.2%	24.0%	17.9%	18.6%	19.0%
Q3		16.0%	17.6%	15.0%	12.2%	20.7%
Q4		20.4%	22.3%	16.9%	22.3%	18.6%
Q5		23.7%	16.9%	37.2%	14.9%	26.0%
All HHs		100.0%	100.0%	100.0%	100.0%	100.0%
As a Share of Income before a Particular Inter-household Transaction						
Q1		18.7%	10.3%	4.5%	3.9%	
Q2		17.5%	10.6%	5.1%	1.8%	
Q3		12.1%	7.1%	3.9%	1.1%	
Q4		17.2%	10.0%	4.9%	2.3%	
Q5		14.2%	5.4%	7.7%	1.1%	
All HHs		15.6%	8.4%	5.4%	1.9%	

Source: Public/Private Transfers and Social Capital, World Bank, 2003.

TABLE A6F: RURAL INTER-HOUSEHOLD TRANSACTIONS INFLOWS (IN LEI AND PERCENTAGES)

Quintile	Number of HHs	Inter-household Transaction	Gift	Payment	Exchange	Income before Inter-household Transaction
Q1	368	4,381,226	1,682,712	1,657,661	1,040,853	25,600,000
Q2	248	5,417,541	2,649,346	1,710,558	1,057,637	46,300,000
Q3	184	5,897,290	2,380,557	2,134,395	1,382,338	68,100,000
Q4	143	7,256,406	2,293,198	3,419,834	1,543,374	78,600,000
Q5	107	12,475,681	4,071,692	5,713,762	2,690,227	147,000,000
All HHs	1,050	6,108,101	2,359,901	2,407,024	1,341,176	57,600,000
As a Share of Total Inter-household Transactions						
Q1		100.0%	38.4%	37.8%	23.8%	
Q2		100.0%	48.9%	31.6%	19.5%	
Q3		100.0%	40.4%	36.2%	23.4%	
Q4		100.0%	31.6%	47.1%	21.3%	
Q5		100.0%	32.6%	45.8%	21.6%	
All HHs		100.0%	38.6%	39.4%	22.0%	
As a Share of a Particular Inter-household Transaction						
Q1		25.1%	25.0%	24.1%	27.2%	15.6%
Q2		20.9%	26.5%	16.8%	18.6%	19.0%
Q3		16.9%	17.7%	15.5%	18.1%	20.7%
Q4		16.2%	13.2%	19.3%	15.7%	18.6%
Q5		20.8%	17.6%	24.2%	20.4%	26.0%
All HHs		100.0%	100.0%	100.0%	100.0%	100.0%
As a Share of Income before Inter-household Transaction						
Q1		17.1%	6.6%	6.5%	4.1%	
Q2		11.7%	5.7%	3.7%	2.3%	
Q3		8.7%	3.5%	3.1%	2.0%	
Q4		9.2%	2.9%	4.4%	2.0%	
Q5		8.5%	2.8%	3.9%	1.8%	
All HHs		10.6%	4.1%	4.2%	2.3%	

Source: Public/Private Transfers and Social Capital Survey, World Bank, 2003.

TABLE A8A: URBAN NET INFORMAL INTER-HOUSEHOLD TRANSACTIONS

Household Type		Net Informal Inter-household Transaction	Gift	Payment	Exchanges	Total Income before Inter Household Transaction
Q1	lei	846,877	780,529	−189,068	255,415	32,500,000
	# of HHs	148	141	69	77	150
Q2	lei	−1,740,940	−1,218,222	−504,952	−17,766	58,000,000
	# of HHs	262	256	105	108	270
Q3	lei	−2,171,280	−1,739,253	−465,789	33,762	72,500,000
	# of HHs	319	311	142	144	334
Q4	lei	−1,867,191	−127,232	−2,073,786	333,827	91,900,000
	# of HHs	357	348	130	134	375
Q5	lei	−7,955,528	−4,249,102	−3,414,630	−291,796	176,000,000
	# of HHs	392	386	188	157	411
All HHs	lei	−3,271,526	−1,679,769	−1,624,256	32,499	98,400,000
	# of HHs	1,478	1,442	634	620	1540
As a Share of Each Transaction, by Quintile						
Q1	% lei	−2.5%	−4.5%	1.1%	76.5%	3.2%
	% of HHs	10.0%	9.8%	10.9%	12.4%	9.7%
Q2	% lei	9.3%	12.7%	5.5%	−9.6%	10.3%
	% of HHs	17.7%	17.8%	16.6%	17.4%	17.5%
Q3	% lei	14.4%	22.5%	6.2%	22.5%	16.0%
	% of HHs	21.6%	21.6%	22.4%	23.2%	21.7%
Q4	% lei	13.9%	1.8%	31.1%	250.1%	22.7%
	% of HHs	24.2%	24.1%	20.5%	21.6%	24.4%
Q5	% lei	64.9%	67.5%	56.1%	−239.6%	47.7%
	% of HHs	26.5%	26.8%	29.7%	25.3%	26.7%
All HHs	% lei	100%	100%	100%	100%	100%
	% of HHs	100%	100%	100%	100%	100%
As a Share of Total Income before a Particular Inter-household Transaction						
Q1	% lei	2.6%	2.4%	−0.6%	0.8%	100%
	% of HHs	98.7%	94.0%	46.0%	51.3%	100%
Q2	% lei	−3.0%	−2.1%	−0.9%	0.0%	100%
	% of HHs	97.0%	94.8%	38.9%	40.0%	100%
Q3	% lei	−3.0%	−2.4%	−0.6%	0.0%	100%
	% of HHs	95.5%	93.1%	42.5%	43.1%	100%
Q4	% lei	−2.0%	−0.1%	−2.3%	0.4%	100%
	% of HHs	95.2%	92.8%	34.7%	35.7%	100%
Q5	% lei	−4.5%	−2.4%	−1.9%	−0.2%	100%
	% of HHs	95.4%	93.9%	45.7%	38.2%	100%
All HHs	% lei	−3.3%	−1.7%	−1.7%	0.0%	100%
	% of HHs	96.0%	93.6%	41.2%	40.3%	100%

Source: Public/Private Transfers and Social Capital Survey, World Bank, 2003.

TABLE A8B: RURAL NET INFORMAL INTER-HOUSEHOLD TRANSACTIONS

Q1	lei	−400,785	−954,756	504,946	49,024	25,600,000
	# of HHs	356	341	269	248	368
Q2	lei	−2,672,976	−2,236,432	−637,881	201,337	46,300,000
	# of HHs	244	236	183	164	248
Q3	lei	−2,337,611	−2,446,898	−517,630	626,917	68,100,000
	# of HHs	177	170	131	103	184
Q4	lei	−6,242,983	−5,588,271	−419,664	−235,047	78,600,000
	# of HHs	141	136	114	108	143
Q5	lei	−8,393,263	−3,931,704	−5,560,537	1,098,978	147,000,000
	# of HHs	106	98	78	77	107
All HHs	lei	−2,886,985	−2,453,362	−688,198	254,575	57,600,000
	# of HHs	1,024	981	775	700	1050

As a Share of Each Transaction, by Quintile

Q1	lei	4.9%	13.6%	−25.7%	6.7%	15.6%
	# of HHs	34.8%	34.8%	34.7%	35.4%	35.0%
Q2	lei	21.9%	21.5%	21.9%	18.7%	19.0%
	# of HHs	23.8%	24.1%	23.6%	23.4%	23.6%
Q3	lei	14.2%	17.5%	13.2%	43.2%	20.7%
	# of HHs	17.3%	17.3%	16.9%	14.7%	17.5%
Q4	lei	29.5%	31.0%	8.3%	−12.6%	18.6%
	# of HHs	13.8%	13.9%	14.7%	15.4%	13.6%
Q5	lei	29.6%	16.3%	82.3%	44.0%	26.0%
	# of HHs	10.4%	10.0%	10.1%	11.0%	10.2%
All HHs	lei	100%	100%	100%	100%	100%
	# of HHs	100%	100%	100%	100%	100%

As a Share of Total Income before a Particular Inter-household Transaction

Q1	% lei	−1.6%	−3.7%	2.0%	0.2%	100%
	% of HHs	96.7%	92.7%	73.1%	67.4%	100%
Q2	% lei	−5.8%	−4.8%	−1.4%	0.4%	100%
	% of HHs	98.4%	95.2%	73.8%	66.1%	100%
Q3	% lei	−3.4%	−3.6%	−0.8%	0.9%	100%
	% of HHs	96.2%	92.4%	71.2%	56.0%	100%
Q4	% lei	−7.9%	−7.1%	−0.5%	−0.3%	100%
	% of HHs	98.6%	95.1%	79.7%	75.5%	100%
Q5	% lei	−5.7%	−2.7%	−3.8%	0.7%	100%
	% of HHs	99.1%	91.6%	72.9%	72.0%	100%
All HHs	% lei	−5.0%	−4.3%	−1.2%	0.4%	100%
	% of HHs	97.5%	93.4%	73.8%	66.7%	100%

Source: Public/Private Transfers and Social Capital Survey, World Bank, 2003.

TABLE A8E: NET INFORMAL LENDING—URBAN (IN LEI AND PERCENTAGES)

Household Type		Mean Value of Transaction	As a Share of Inter-household Transaction by Quintile	As a Share of Total Income Before Inter-household Transaction
Q1	lei	−33,267	2.3%	−0.1%
	# of HHs	82	19.2%	54.7%
Q2	lei	2,778	−0.3%	0.0%
	# of HHs	147	20.1%	54.4%
Q3	lei	466,916	−72.7%	0.6%
	# of HHs	169	19.0%	50.6%
Q4	lei	−645,547	112.8%	−0.7%
	# of HHs	198	20.2%	52.8%
Q5	lei	−302,350	57.9%	−0.2%
	# of HHs	231	21.5%	56.2%
All HHs	lei	−139,374	100%	−0.1%
	# of HHs	827	100%	53.7%

Urban Informal Lending (Outflows and Inflows)

	Outflows				Inflows			
Quintile	# of HHs	Loan Amount	As a Share of an Inter-household Transaction by Quintile	As a Share of Income before Inter-household Transaction	# of HHs	Loan Amount	As a Share of an Inter-household Transaction by Quintile	As a Share of Income before Inter-household Transaction
Q1	150	1,327,667	4.2%	4.1%	150	1,294,400	4.3%	4.0%
Q2	270	1,530,556	8.7%	2.6%	270	1,533,333	9.1%	2.6%
Q3	334	1,609,281	11.3%	2.2%	334	2,076,198	15.3%	2.9%
Q4	334	2,609,093	18.4%	2.8%	334	1,963,547	14.5%	2.1%
Q5	375	6,356,000	50.3%	3.6%	375	6,053,650	50.2%	3.4%
All HHs	1,540	3,078,329	100.0%	3.1%	1,540	2,938,955	100.0%	3.0%

Source: Public/Private Transfers and Social Capital Survey, World Bank, 2003.

TABLE A8F: NET INFORMAL LENDING—RURAL (IN LEI AND PERCENTAGES)

Household Type		Mean Value of Transaction	As a Share of Inter-household Transaction by Quintile	As a Share of Total Income before Inter-household Transaction
Q1	lei	−224,389	22.9%	−0.9%
	# of HHs	181	33.5%	49.2%
Q2	lei	−301,331	20.7%	−0.7%
	# of HHs	128	23.7%	51.6%
Q3	lei	−128,370	6.5%	−0.2%
	# of HHs	91	16.8%	49.5%
Q4	lei	520,874	−20.7%	0.7%
	# of HHs	78	14.4%	54.5%
Q5	lei	−2,376,168	70.5%	−1.6%
	# of HHs	63	11.6%	58.9%
All HHs	lei	−343,514	100%	−0.6%
	# of HHs	541	100%	51.5%

Rural Informal Lending (Outflows and Inflows)

	Outflows				Inflows			
Quintile	# of HHs	Loan Amount	As a Share of an Inter-household Transaction by Quintile	As a Share of Income before Inter-household Transaction	# of HHs	Loan Amount	As a Share of an Inter-household Transaction by Quintile	As a Share of Income before Inter-household Transaction
Q1	368	761,182	14.2%	3.0%	368	536,794	12.3%	2.1%
Q2	248	1,439,315	18.1%	3.1%	248	1,137,984	17.5%	2.5%
Q3	184	1,242,120	11.6%	1.8%	184	1,113,750	12.7%	1.6%
Q4	143	1,493,986	10.8%	1.9%	143	2,014,860	17.9%	2.6%
Q5	107	8,335,047	45.2%	5.7%	107	5,958,879	39.6%	4.1%
All HHs	1,050	1,877,243	100.0%	3.3%	1,050	1,533,729	100.0%	2.7%

Source: Public/Private Transfers and Social Capital Survey, World Bank, 2003.

TABLE A9: SELECTED CHARACTERISTICS OF ROMANIAN HOUSEHOLDS BY PRIVATE TRANSFER STATUS

	Number	Percentage
Households Giving Only	381	14.70%
Households Giving Only (urban)	276	17.47%
Households Giving Only (rural)	105	10.38%
Households Receiving Only	42	1.62%
Households Receiving Only (urban)	32	2.03%
Households Receiving Only (Rural)	10	0.99%
Households Both Giving and Receiving	2103	81.13%
Households Both Giving and Receiving (urban)	1218	77.09%
Households Both Giving and Receiving (rural)	885	87.45%
Households Neither Giving Nor Receiving	66	2.55%
Households Neither Giving Nor Receiving (urban)	54	3.42%
Households Neither Giving Nor Receiving (rural)	12	1.19%
Total	2592	100%
Urban	1580	100%
Rural	1012	100%
Net Transfer Donors	1545	59.61%
Urban	912	57.72%
Rural	633	62.55%
Net Transfer Recipients	963	37.15%
Urban	605	38.29%
Rural	358	35.38%
Net Transfer Equals Zero (Others)	84	3.24%
Urban	63	3.99%
Rural	21	2.08%
Total	2592	100%
Urban	1580	100%
Rural	1012	100%

Table A9: Selected Characteristics of Romanian Households by Private Transfer Status (Continued)				

Welfare Variables	All Households	Net Transfer Donors	Net Transfer Recipients	Others
Total Household Income (surs I—99) mean in lei	67,200,000	69,500,000	64,300,000	59,700,000
Urban	83,200,000	87,700,000	77,800,000	67,900,000
Rural	42,400,000	43,100,000	41,500,000	35,200,000
MIG Received (lei)	822,998	736,669	981,362	595,298
Urban	719,275	622,092	927,441	127,064
Rural	984,936	901,746	1,072,486	2,000,000
Non-MIG Received (lei)	1,176,274	873,120	1,342,724	4,843,929
Urban	1,448,751	1,053,869	1,538,205	6,306,103
Rural	750,866	612,704	1,012,372	457,409
Consumption (per adult per day in $)(mean)	3.60	3.53	3.71	3.60
Urban	4.29	4.28	4.32	4.23
Rural	2.52	2.46	2.69	1.70
Assets (number of durable goods)	9.20	9.37	8.94	8.83
Urban	10.5	10.75	10.2	9.9
Rural	7.16	7.39	6.82	5.62
Satisfaction of Financial Situation (1–10)	4.06	4.16	3.93	3.76
Urban	4.13	4.27	3.94	4.05
Rural	3.95	4	3.93	2.9
Percentage of in good health	55.07%	56.33%	52.45%	61.90%
Urban	61.45%	63.56%	58.37%	60.32%
Rural	45.09%	45.87%	42.46%	66.67%
HH Characteristics				
Age of the Subject	52.23	52.12	52.21	54.49
Urban	50.56	51.02	49.47	54.44
Rural	54.83	53.70	56.83	54.62
Percentage of Female Headed HH	15.93%	13.46%	20.46%	9.52%
Urban	15.32%	14.14%	17.85%	7.94%
Rural	16.90%	12.48%	24.86%	14.29%
Percentage of HH with Pensioner Present	59.10%	59.09%	58.77%	63.10%
Urban	53.61%	54.93%	51.07%	58.73%
Rural	67.69%	65.09%	71.79%	76.19%
HH size (number of Individuals)	3.03	3.12	2.91	2.9
Urban	3.00	3.05	2.96	2.81
Rural	3.08	3.21	2.84	3.19

(Continued)

TABLE A9: Selected Characteristics of Romanian Households by Private Transfer Status (Continued)

Welfare Variables	All Households	Net Transfer Donors	Net Transfer Recipients	Others
Multigenerational	18.09%	18.12%	17.86%	20.24%
Urban	14.75%	15.13%	14.21%	14.29%
Rural	23.32%	22.43%	24.02%	38.10%
Number of Children (under 18)	0.61	0.63	0.61	0.38
Urban	0.58	0.57	0.61	0.38
Rural	0.66	0.70	0.61	0.38
Social Capital				
Percentage of trustpeop =1	37.03%	36.78%	37.01%	41.67%
Urban	36.08%	36.26%	35.27%	41.27%
Rural	38.52%	37.54%	40.00%	42.86%
Percentage of trustnei =1	57.98%	58.54%	57.39%	54.32%
Urban	60.51%	61.29%	59.72%	56.67%
Rural	54.11%	54.65%	53.54%	47.62%
Percentage of helppoor =1(cs2_c =1or2)	65.13%	65.42%	65.30%	57.69%
Urban	64.65%	64.71%	65.54%	55.17%
Rural	65.85%	66.39%	64.91%	65.00%
Relation (average of cs5)	0.209	0.211	0.210	0.156
Urban	0.193	0.196	0.192	0.163
Rural	0.233	0.233	0.239	0.133
Number of close friends (cs6)	8.208	8.396	8.086	6.159
Urban	7.669	8.075	7.293	5.452
Rural	9.067	8.863	9.479	8.35
Amount of Help (no. of Yes to WS1–WS6)	1.838	1.864	1.853	1.19
Urban	2.062	2.13	2.031	1.365
Rural	1.488	1.48	1.55	0.667
Collective Action and Cooperation				
Cooperation(alpha index of ac5)	0.0013	0.0047	0.0006	−0.0534
Urban	0.0079	0.0103	0.0117	−0.0625
Rural	−0.0090	−0.0034	−0.0181	−0.0261
Groups and Networks				
Number of memberships in different org.	1.076	1.0460	1.0620	1.7857
Urban	1.2076	1.1732	1.1802	1.9683
Rural	0.8706	0.8626	0.8631	1.2381
Education of the HH subject				
No education	1.31%	1.23%	1.35%	2.38%
Urban	0.63%	0.88%	0.33%	0.00%
Rural	2.37%	1.74%	3.07%	9.52%

TABLE A9: SELECTED CHARACTERISTICS OF ROMANIAN HOUSEHOLDS BY PRIVATE TRANSFER STATUS (CONTINUED)

Welfare Variables	All Households	Net Transfer Donors	Net Transfer Recipients	Others
Primary + Secondary School	31.63%	31.28%	31.95%	34.52%
Urban	16.87%	15.81%	17.58%	25.40%
Rural	54.64%	53.55%	56.15%	61.90%
Professional School	16.61%	17.03%	16.23%	13.10%
Urban	17.82%	18.00%	17.91%	14.29%
Rural	14.72%	15.64%	13.41%	9.52%
High School	28.58%	28.56%	28.82%	26.19%
Urban	33.29%	33.59%	33.33%	28.57%
Rural	21.25%	21.33%	21.23%	19.05%
Post High School and Above	21.95%	21.94%	21.81%	23.81%
Urban	31.52%	31.80%	31.07%	31.75%
Rural	7.02%	7.74%	6.15%	0.00%
Transfers				
Net Transfer Donors	59.61%	100.00%	0.00%	0.00%
Urban	57.72%	100.00%	0.00%	0.00%
Rural	62.55%	100.00%	0.00%	0.00%
Net Transfer Receivers	37.15%	0.00%	100.00%	0.00%
Urban	38.29%	0.00%	100.00%	0.00%
Rural	35.38%	0.00%	100.00%	0.00%
Others	3.24%	0.00%	0.00%	100.00%
Urban	3.99%	0.00%	0.00%	100.00%
Rural	2.08%	0.00%	0.00%	100.00%
Giving Transfer Only	14.70%	(328) 21.23%	(52) 5.40%	(1) 1.19%
Urban	17.47%	(253) 27.74%	(23) 3.80%	(0) 0.00%
Rural	10.38%	(75) 11.85%	(29) 8.10%	(1) 4.76%
Receiving Transfer Only	1.62%	(4) 0.26%	(38) 3.95%	(0) 0%
Urban	2.03%	(1) 0.11%	(31) 5.12%	(0) 0%
Rural	0.99%	(3) 0.47%	(7) 1.96%	(0) 0.00%
Both Receiving and Giving	81.13%	(1213) 78.51%	(873) 90.65%	(17) 20.24
Urban	77.09%	(658) 72.25%	(551) 91.07%	(9) 14.29%
Rural	87.45%	(555) 87.68%	(322) 89.94%	(8) 38.10%
Neither Receiving Nor Giving	2.55%	(0) 0.00%	(0) 0%	(66) 78.57
Urban	3.42%	(0) 0%	(0) 0.00%	(54) 85.71%
Rural	1.19%	(0) 0%	(0) 0.00%	(12) 57.14%
Gross Transfers Given (lei)	12,700,000	14,400,000	11,000,000	843,095
Urban	13,800,000	15,900,000	12,100,000	701,587
Rural	11,000,000	12,300,000	9,128,058	1,267,619
Gross Transfers Received (lei)	9,441,074	5,819,674	16,000,000	620,476
Urban	10,600,000	5,205,713	19,900,000	576,191
Rural	7,568,862	6,704,244	9,497,435	753,333

(Continued)

TABLE A9: SELECTED CHARACTERISTICS OF ROMANIAN HOUSEHOLDS BY PRIVATE TRANSFER STATUS (CONTINUED)

Welfare Variables	All Households	Net Transfer Donors	Net Transfer Recipients	Others
Net Transfers (lei)	−1,257,341	−10,100,000	12,800,000	0
Urban	−469,971	−11,400,000	15,900,000	0
Rural	−2,486,633	−8,266,835	7,587,803	0
Sample Size	(100%) 2592	(100%) 1545	(100%) 963	(100%) 84
Urban	(100%) 1580	(100%) 912	(100%) 605	(100%) 63
Rural	(100%) 1012	(100%) 638	(100%) 358	(100%) 21

Note: In 2002, the average exchange rate was 33,055.40 lei per US dollar.

Source: Public/Private Transfers and Social Capital Survey, World Bank, 2003.

MULTIVARIATE ANALYSES

Table B1 presents multivariate tests of determinants of gross inflows from inter-household transactions. Inflows include gifts or loans received, and payment in cash or in kind for goods and services provided. In equation 1, the dependent variable is inflows in millions of lei.[13]

Number of adults in the household is significantly associated with reduced inflows in equation 1. This finding has a highly intuitive explanation. Many inter-household transactions, particularly for gifts or loans, occur across generations of the same family. Where they are in the same household already, any such transactions will not show up in the data. Number of children is associated with higher inflows, although this relationship is only of marginal statistical significance.

Age (of respondent) is related to inter-household transfers in the usual way. As age increases, gross inflows fall and then eventually rise again (beyond about age 67). Higher income-earners and wealthier households (measured by types of assets owned) have significantly higher inflows, controlling for other variables. Landowners have higher inflows, while homeowners had somewhat lower inflows.[14]

MIG assistance (cash benefits, means-tested heating subsidies, and emergency relief) is positively but not significantly related to inflows. However, other social assistance income is strongly associated with higher inflows. These results are consistent with the possibility that public assistance does not "crowd out" private transfers, or other income from inter-household transactions. However, the regression coefficients could be capturing both a (negative) "crowd out" effect and a (positive) effect of otherwise unobserved characteristics associated with need.

---

13. Because the dependent variable is truncated at 0, and there are quite a few 0 values (447 households have 0 gross inflows), we use tobit regression. T-statistics are in parentheses below the corresponding regression coefficients.

14. In other tests, number of hectares owned had no relationship to inflows (or outflows).

Only by controlling fully for a household's need for private assistance, with variables other than MIG assistance, could we confidently attribute the MIG coefficient to the effects of "crowd out" or absence of "crowd out."

The presence of a pensioner in the household is associated with lower inflows, at least in urban areas. Rural residence makes no difference for households without pensioners. However, rural households with pensioners receive significantly higher inflows, relative to rural households without a pensioner or to urban households with pensioners. (Rural pensioner is an interaction term equal to the product of the two dummy variables "rural" and "pensioner.") This result is consistent with the fact that most pensioners in rural areas receive CAP pensions, which are far less lucrative than the standard state old age pension received by most pensioners in urban areas.

A "public activism" index was constructed from five questions on attending public meetings, participating in protests, participating in election meetings, alerting media to a local problem, and notifying the police or courts about a local problem. Activists are likely to be better integrated socially into the community, and are also likely to have a stronger sense of initiative. Therefore, this index could be associated with higher inflows and outflows. To the extent that activism reflects altruism, it could be associated more strongly with outflows than with inflows. Equation 1 (Table B1) shows that households with civic activists have higher inflows than other households.

Equation 2 analyzes the determinants of whether or not a household receives positive gross inflows, while equation 3 analyzes the level of inflows only for those households with positive inflows. The dependent variable in equation 2 takes on the value 0 for households reporting no inflows, and the value 1 for those reporting some inflows (82.7 percent of the households in the sample). Probit regression is therefore used. Coefficients in the table indicate marginal effects evaluated at the means of all other independent variables.

An additional adult in the household reduces the likelihood of receiving some inflows by 3 percentage points. Age affects the probability of receiving inflows in the same curvilinear fashion as displayed in equation 1. Income, assets, and owning a home have no impact. Landowners are more likely to receive positive inflows. Social assistance, including MIG, has no effect. Pensioners reduce the probability of a household receiving inflows by 6 percentage points.

Equation 3 analyzes, using OLS, the determinants of inflows conditional on receiving positive inflows. The sample for this regression therefore excludes the 447 households reporting 0 inflows. Number of adults reduces inflows. The effect of age is curvilinear as in equations 1 and 2. The amount of inflows increases with income, assets, and land ownership, and decreases with home ownership. Pensioners are found to reduce the size of inflows in equation 3, as they did the likelihood of inflows in equation 2. Rural residence is unrelated to the size of inflows for non-pensioners, but rural pensioners have significantly larger inflows, as do public activists.[15]

Table B2 shows the results of similar tests of the determinants of outflows, measured by gifts and loans provided, and by cash and in-kind payments for goods and services received. Equations 1-3 are perfectly analogous to the same-numbered equations in Table B1.

Number of adults and number of children are related to outflows in Table B2 (equation 1) in the same way they were to inflows in Table B1. The most striking difference between Tables 1 and 2 is the lack of any significant effect of age on outflows. Income, assets and land ownership are positively related to outflows, as they were to inflows. Home ownership is negatively related to outflows in Table B2, as it was to inflows in Table B1.

Social assistance other than MIG is positively related to outflows. Outflows are lower for households with pensioners. Outflows (but not inflows, in Table B1) are significantly higher for rural households, particularly for those with pensioners. Public activism is associated with higher outflows, as it is for inflows.

---

15. Activism does not have discernible "external" effects on inter-household transactions: community-level means of activism were insignificant when added to any of the regressions in Table 1.

TABLE B1: INTER-HOUSEHOLD TRANSACTIONS GROSS INFLOWS REGRESSIONS

Equation	1	2	3
Transfers Variable	Gross Inflows	Gross Inflows > 0	Gross Inflows (if > 0)
Method	Tobit	Probit	OLS
Intercept	−16.306	—	−25.097
	(−1.41)		(−1.60)
Number of adults in household	−3.022	−.0297	−2.318
	(−5.11)	(−2.87)	(−3.68)
Number of children	1.015	.0151	0.556
	(1.62)	(1.35)	(0.91)
Age of subject	−0.897	−.0087	−0.720
	(−4.07)	(−2.50)	(−4.59)
Age squared	0.006	.0001	0.005
	(3.07)	(1.78)	(3.96)
Log of income (excl. transfers)	2.988	−.0189	3.268
	(4.66)	(−1.47)	(3.11)
Asset index	0.471	−.0003	0.624
	(3.13)	(−0.09)	(3.44)
Owns land	5.333	.0478	4.126
	(4.18)	(2.21)	(2.47)
Owns home	−2.688	−.0154	−2.498
	(−1.75)	(−0.70)	(−1.74)
MIG cash income	0.186	.0031	0.150
	(1.60)	(1.16)	(1.78)
Other social assistance	0.362	−.0009	1.086
	(6.38)	(−1.24)	(1.88)
Pensioner in household	−4.452	−.0579	−3.047
	(−2.28)	(−2.30)	(−2.39)
Rural	−0.821	.0516	−2.144
	(−0.53)	(1.54)	(−1.33)
Rural pensioner	5.033	.0339	3.543
	(2.19)	(0.93)	(2.42)
Public activism index	2.074	.0156	2.062
	(2.45)	(1.24)	(1.95)
Regression stat.	Chi^2=249.7	chi^2=81.2	R^2=.15
N	2590	2590	2143

All dependent variables are in millions of lei. T or Z statistics are in parentheses. Probit coefficients are marginal effects evaluated at mean of all other regressors.

Source: Public/Private Transfers and Social Capital, World Bank, 2003.

TABLE B2: INTER-HOUSEHOLD TRANSACTIONS GROSS OUTFLOWS AND NET INFLOWS REGRESSIONS

Equation	1	2	3	4
Transfers Variable	Gross Outflows	Gross Outflows > 0	Gross Outflows (if > 0)	Net Inflows
Method	Tobit	Probit	OLS	OLS
Intercept	−78.485	—	−74.501	52.389
	(−5.78)	—	(−3.20)	(3.39)
Number of adults in household	−3.236	−.0014	−3.237	0.967
	(−4.74)	(−0.43)	(−3.67)	(1.07)
Number of children	1.335	.0029	1.227	−0.567
	(1.83)	(0.75)	(1.22)	(−0.62)
Age of subject	0.128	.0004	0.140	−0.848
	(0.50)	(0.29)	(0.70)	(−3.93)
Age squared	−0.002	−.0001	−0.002	0.007
	(−.62)	(−0.57)	(−0.85)	(3.69)
Log of income (excl. transfers)	4.720	.0026	4.576	−1.470
	(6.29)	(0.80)	(3.01)	(−1.39)
Asset index	1.387	.0029	1.338	−0.863
	(7.96)	(2.86)	(3.49)	(−2.38)
Owns land	3.085	.0146	2.480	1.304
	(2.09)	(1.43)	(1.93)	(0.87)
Owns home	−3.662	.0055	−3.984	1.533
	(−2.04)	(0.51)	(−2.29)	(0.96)
MIG cash income	0.104	.0001	0.100	0.049
	(0.77)	(0.13)	(1.45)	(0.56)
Other social assistance	0.158	−.0005	0.567	0.187
	(2.31)	(−2.85)	(3.48)	(0.80)
Pensioner in household	−4.584	−.0245	−3.416	0.991
	(−2.04)	(−2.22)	(−2.53)	(0.93)
Rural	3.620	.0276	3.039	−4.701
	(2.00)	(2.25)	(1.14)	(−1.68)
Rural pensioner	4.187	.0147	2.939	0.478
	(1.58)	(1.06)	(1.35)	(0.19)
Public activism index	2.320	.0026	2.366	−0.630
	(2.35)	(0.39)	(1.87)	(−0.62)
Regression statistic	chi^2=257.5	chi^2=156.2	R^2=.10	R^2=.02
N	2590	2590	2482	2590

All dependent variables are in millions of lei. T or Z statistics are in parentheses. A ** and * indicate significance at .01 and .05 respectively for 2-tailed tests. Probit coefficients are marginal effects evaluated at mean of all other regressors.

Source: Public/Private Transfers and Social Capital, World Bank, 2003.

The likelihood of positive gross outflows (equation 2) is higher for rural households and for households with more assets, and is lower for households with pensioners or which receive social assistance other than MIG. Equation 3 analyzes the level of outflows, for the 2,482 households (all but 108) with positive outflows. Outflows increase with income, assets, landowning, public activism, and receipts of non-MIG social assistance. They decrease with number of adults in the household, home ownership, and pensioners in the household.

Equation 4 of Table B2 analyzes net inflows using OLS. The dependent variable is gross inflows minus gross outflows. While gross inflows and outflows are a measure of involvement in inter-household transactions, net inflows are more a measure of transfers: where net inflows are high, households are getting more than they are giving. Most studies of private transfers in other countries have found they redistribute income in a progressive manner, i.e. from richer to poorer households. Equation 4, however, shows that, controlling for other determinants of net inflows, income is unrelated to net inflows: private transfers are distribution-neutral. Asset ownership is significantly related to lower net inflows in equation 4, showing some evidence of progressivity. Net inflows are lower for rural than for urban households, however. Age has its commonly-observed quadratic pattern in equation 4, indicating transfers in net are from the middle-aged to the young and old.

Net inflows are unrelated to receipt of MIG or other social assistance. This result suggests no "crowding in" or "crowding out" of private transfers by public assistance, but we cannot rule out "crowd out" effects for the reasons explained above.[16]

Table B3 shows determinants of MIG assistance (cash benefits, means-tested heating subsidies, and emergency relief), in millions of lei. Tobit regression is used because the dependent variable is truncated at 0. Only 424 of the 2,521 households in the sample received MIG assistance. Social assistance, inter-household transfers and local revenues per capita are all in millions of lei. Equation 1 analyzes the determinants of MIG assistance for all households, urban and rural. Equations 2 and 3 respectively divide the sample into urban and rural sub-samples. Equations 4 and 5 include all households, but separate MIG assistance into its two main components—cash benefits (equation 4) and heating subsidies (equation 5).

In all equations, MIG assistance is unrelated to the volume of inter-household transfers: neither inflows nor outflows are significantly associated with MIG. Net inflows (inflows minus outflows) are also unrelated to MIG, when substituted (in results not shown) for inflows and outflows. Potentially, inflows converted to assets could still reduce MIG assistance through the significant assets variable in the regression. However, the inter-household transactions variables all remain insignificant when the assets variables are omitted from the model. Further tests not reported in the table divided urban from rural households, and found no evidence in either sub-sample that inter-household transactions affected MIG assistance.

These results are consistent with the possibility that private transfers do not "crowd out" public assistance, neither by reducing the likelihood a household applies for MIG nor by affecting its eligibility. However, these coefficients could be capturing both a (negative) "crowd out" effect and the (positive) effect of otherwise unobserved characteristics associated with need. Only if we could control fully for a household's need for public assistance, with variables other than inter-household transfers, could we confidently attribute the inter-household transfer coefficients to the effects of "crowd out" or absence of "crowd out."

Age (of respondent) is also unrelated to MIG assistance in all equations in Table B3 (and remains insignificant when a linear function of age is substituted for the quadratic). Households with more children receive significantly more MIG benefits, controlling for other variables. This result holds for the full sample (equation 1), for urban households (equation 2), for rural

---

16. Results in these tables are not sensitive to outliers. Dropping the most extreme cases of reported inflows and outflows – some of which seem implausibly high – does not materially alter any findings reported here.

TABLE B3: MIG TRANSFERS REGRESSIONS

Equation	1	2	3	4	5
Sample	All	Urban	Rural	All	All
MIG category	All	All	All	Cash benefits	Heating Subsidies
Intercept	4.513	0.061	7.163	−14.072	−0.826
	(0.72)	(0.01)	(0.46)	(−1.84)	(−0.36)
Gross inter-hh inflows	0.010	0.006	0.046	0.009	0.003
	(1.17)	(1.15)	(0.66)	(0.95)	(0.93)
Gross inter-hh outflows	−0.019	−0.010	−0.151	−0.005	−0.011
	(−1.21)	(−1.03)	(−1.19)	(−0.32)	(−1.29)
Age of subject	0.055	0.122	−0.351	−0.015	0.045
	(0.36)	(1.08)	(−0.80)	(−0.09)	(0.79)
Age squared	−0.001	−0.001	0.002	−0.001	−0.001
	(−0.39)	(−0.93)	(0.55)	(−0.23)	(−0.53)
Number of children	2.188	1.568	2.728	1.945	0.582
	(5.01)	(4.82)	(2.27)	(4.11)	(3.57)
Log of income (excl. transfers)	−1.044	−0.667	−1.131	−0.230	−0.264
	(−4.06)	(−2.75)	(−1.95)	(−0.70)	(−2.81)
MIG-relevant Assets	−1.354	−0.809	−1.858	−1.220	−0.371
	(−4.22)	(−3.56)	(−1.82)	(−3.35)	(−3.06)
Non-MIG-relevant assets	−0.188	−0.099	−0.973	−0.251	−0.155
	(−0.92)	(−0.67)	(−1.55)	(−1.08)	(−2.01)
Owns land	−2.410	−1.089	−4.699	−1.460	−0.988
	(−2.38)	(−1.46)	(−1.64)	(−1.28)	(−2.57)
Locally-raised revenues p.c.	5.082	2.620	3.154	3.840	1.508
	(3.85)	(2.65)	(0.54)	(2.66)	(3.05)
Public activism (locality mean)	6.962	7.751	8.295	2.122	2.978
	(2.41)	(2.81)	(1.24)	(0.67)	(2.48)
Tenure in office of mayor	0.834	0.336	1.463	0.082	0.312
	(6.54)	(3.27)	(3.50)	(0.57)	(6.20)
PSD mayor	2.086	0.302	5.099	−0.452	0.988
	(2.35)	(0.43)	(1.87)	(−0.45)	(2.88)
Poor influence local decisions	1.865	0.148	1.234	−0.842	0.705
	(2.79)	(0.20)	(0.79)	(−1.11)	(2.50)
Percent Roma	−74.327	−44.445	−91.692	5.184	−20.005
	(−3.78)	(−1.28)	(−2.27)	(0.25)	(−2.30)
Rural	0.045	—	—	1.838	−2.595
	(0.03)			(1.20)	(−4.58)
pseudo R^2	.04	.05	.05	.03	.10
Observations	2521	1529	992	2521	2521
Observations > 0	424	299	125	210	250
Mean, dep. var.	0.819	0.699	1.001	0.451	0.159

Method is tobit regression. Dependent variable is MIG assistance received, in millions of lei. Inter-household transfers and local government revenues are also measured in millions of lei. T statistics are in parentheses.

Source: Public/Private Transfers and Social Capital, World Bank, 2003.

households (equation 3), and separately for MIG cash benefits (equation 4) and heating subsidies (equation 5). Benefits are supposed to be based in part on number of children, so these findings are unsurprising, although still reassuring.

Higher income (per adult equivalent, measured exclusive of inter-household transactions and social assistance) is associated with significantly lower MIG receipts, for the full sample (equation 1), for urban households (equation 2), and rural households (equation 3). Surprisingly, MIG cash benefits are unrelated to income (equation 4), although heating subsidies are higher for lower-income households (equation 5).

Households with more assets also receive lower MIG benefits. Asset types were divided into two categories: 1) goods that are potentially income-producing, or luxury goods, and are generally taken into account when MIG administrators evaluate applicants; and 2) other assets that generally are not considered.[17] As expected, the first type of asset is more strongly associated with reduced MIG benefits than the second type. Land ownership also reduces MIG benefits.[18] The coefficients on income and assets (including land) are higher for the rural sub-sample than for the urban sub-sample, suggesting better targeting in rural areas. Officials in rural areas, despite more limited administrative capacity for investigating applicants, might have more accurate information on their standard of living.

Although there are sizeable earmarked transfers from central government for social assistance, the revenue measure most strongly associated with higher MIG benefits is locally-raised revenues per capita. This variable is significant in four of the five tests (equation 3 for rural households is the exception). Localities are expected to cover about 20 percent of the cost of MIG from local revenues. There is wide variation in locally raised revenues, however, and many localities—particularly smaller and less wealthy localities which are able to raise fewer revenues locally—do not even come close to covering their 20 percent share of costs.

Public activism at the local level could be associated with improved accountability of local government, which must consider the possibility that citizens will protest in various ways if services are inadequate. To the extent local officials have control over MIG funds and implementation, households residing in communities with greater activism may receive higher MIG assistance. A household's own activism matters, however, only to the degree it contributes to the "public good" of monitoring local government. Therefore, a household's own level of activism should be unrelated to MIG assistance, controlling for the mean community level. The household's own level of civic activism turned out to be unrelated to MIG assistance, as expected, and this variable was omitted from the models reported in the tables for space reasons. The community level mean of the index, however, has a positive and significant (in equations 1, 2 and 5) coefficient.

Number of years the mayor has been in office is positively and significantly related to MIG assistance (equation 1). More experienced mayors may be more effective in lobbying higher levels of government for transfers to local government budgets. However, this variable remains significant when those transfers are controlled for. More experienced mayors may administer social assistance programs more effectively, or, alternatively, those who manage to run more successful programs may increase their chances of re-election. Mayoral tenure is positive and significant in the urban (equation 2) and rural (equation 3) sub-samples, and for heating subsidies (equation 5), but not for cash benefits (equation 4).

---

17. The first group includes cars, vans, motorcycles, agricultural equipment, animals, CD players, cell phones, refrigerators, freezers, microwave ovens, computers and internet service, and color television. The second group includes radios, tape players and stereo systems, vacuum cleaners, telephones, cookers and stoves, black and white television, cable TV, video players, book collections, washing machines, sewing machines, and bicycles.

18. In additional tests, home ownership was found to have no impact.

Households residing in localities with PSD mayors receive significantly higher MIG assistance (equation 1). This result holds for households in rural localities (equation 3), where limited locally-raised revenues make town halls more dependent on transfers from central and county government, which is controlled by the PSD. The result does not hold for urban areas, which are less dependent on such transfers. However, the PSD effect remains when transfers from central and county government are controlled for (in additional tests not reported in the table), and those transfers are not significant predictors of MIG benefits received by households. It is therefore somewhat of a mystery why MIG benefits are higher in PSD-governed localities.

Residents of peripheral villages are often thought to be disadvantaged politically, relative to residents of communal centers, where the town hall is located. In tests not reported in the table, no difference was found, however, between MIG assistance levels in central and peripheral villages.

Where poor people have more influence over local government policy, it is natural to expect public assistance to be more generous. A survey of public officials included a question asked about the level of influence poor people (and various other groups) exercised over decisions by the town hall and local council. Where poor people were judged to have more influence, MIG benefits are higher (equation 1). This variable is not significant, however, when the sample is broken down into urban and rural sub-samples (equations 2 and 3). It is a significant predictor of heating subsidies (equation 5), but not of cash benefits (equation 4).

Several studies, mostly based on U.S. data, have found that support for redistribution and provision of public goods is lower in more ethnically heterogeneous communities. In the 51 localities represented in this study, the Roma population in the last census varied from 0 to 11.7 percent, averaging 1.9. The effect of Roma on MIG assistance could be positive (if they tend to be poorer, and their poverty is not fully captured by the other regressors) or negative (if there is less support for assistance where more of it is likely to go to a different ethnic group). Table B3 (equation 1) shows that localities with a higher share of Roma have significantly lower MIG assistance (equation 1). This result is stronger for the rural sub-sample (equation 3) than for the urban sub-sample (equation 2). Moreover, the negative effect of percent Roma holds only for heating subsidies (equation 5), and not for cash assistance (equation 4), when MIG assistance is divided into those two components. In tests not reported in the table, percent Hungarian population (which varies from 0 to 99.3 percent, averaging 10 percent in the 51 localities) showed no consistent relationship with MIG assistance.

It is possible that discrimination could occur within communities. For example, independently of the ethnic composition of the locality in which they live, Roma households could receive lower MIG benefits, controlling for income, assets, and so on. Unfortunately, there is no way to identify Roma households in the data. Hungarian households can be identified, however. Hungarian ethnicity does not significantly lower a household's MIG benefits, even in overwhelmingly non-Hungarian localities.

Controlling for the effects of other variables, cash benefits are somewhat higher for rural households (equation 4), but heating subsidies are larger for urban households (equation 5). The bottom row of the table shows the means of the dependent variables. The average MIG assistance for all households is 819 thousand lei per month (equation 1), but most households receive 0; among the 424 households receiving MIG benefits, the average is 4.87 million. The average is higher for rural than for urban households: 1.001 million compared to 699 thousand. For the full sample, cash benefits averaged 451 thousand (equation 4), and heating subsidies averaged 159 thousand (equation 5).

To summarize, there is very little evidence in these tests that the benefits to the poor from inter-household transactions are offset by accompanying reductions in their public assistance benefits. These tests are not conclusive, however, as they cannot fully control for factors that may affect either eligibility for MIG or gifts and informal loans received. There is some reassuring evidence that MIG works as planned: households with more children, lower incomes, fewer luxury assets or assets with income-producing potential, receive more assistance. Benefits also tend to be

TABLE B4: SOCIAL CAPITAL, ETHNIC FRACTIONALIZATION, AND LOCAL GOVERNMENT PERFORMANCE

Dependent Variable	Client Satisfaction		Trust in the Mayor	
	1	2	3	4
Intercept	28.4	119.2	1.65	6.06
	(0.40)	(1.92)	(0.35)	(1.45)
Expenditures per capita	1.38	1.35	0.02	−0.01
	(3.29)	(3.69)	(0.57)	(−0.38)
Log of locality population	−2.20	−2.02	−0.92	−0.12
	(−2.52)	(−2.40)	(−1.89)	(−2.12)
Log of mean locality income	3.32	−1.46	0.74	−0.07
	(0.77)	(−0.38)	(0.28)	(−0.27)
Neighbor relations index	59.9		3.44	
	(3.17)		(2.68)	
Income inequality	−8.34			
	(−3.25)			
Ethnic fractionalization		−14.1		−.87
		(−2.06)		(−2.14)
R^2	.46	.33	.29	.21
Mean, dep. var.		76.3%		2.88

Sample size is 50. T-ratios are in parentheses.
Source: Public/Private Transfers and Social Capital, World Bank, 2003.

higher where there is more civic activism, and where the poor have more influence over local political decision-making. More unsettling results, however, are the lower level of benefits in localities that raise fewer revenues locally, and higher benefits in localities with mayors from the PSD or who have been in office longer, suggesting that political factors influence allocations. Most disturbing of all, perhaps, is the finding that MIG assistance is lower in communities with a higher share of Roma in the population.

SAMPLE AND SAMPLE METHODOLOGY

The study used *qualitative and quantitative methods* to collect community and household-level data. During the preparatory stage, three focus groups and five open-ended interviews were conducted with rural and urban poor, as well as with public and private service providers.

During the second stage, the following surveys were carried out: a household-level survey and a local officials survey. Seventeen focus groups and individual semi-structured interviews were conducted with poor and non-poor rural and urban inhabitants, local officials, and public and private service providers, as outlined below.

A locality card was filled for each locality enrolled in the sample. The card contained social, demographic, and economic data as well as specific information about budgets and social services provision.

The Household Survey

- *Sample size:* 2,641 households.
- *Sample type:* stratified, probabilistic, three-stage sample.
- *Stratification criteria:* 18 geographic areas based on historical regions, residence (urban-rural), urban locality size (4 types), degree of development of rural localities (3 categories).
- *Sampling:* probabilistic selection of localities (51 total, 27 rural), sample units (streets, 264) and households. Households were selected by random route method.
- Forty households in rural areas and between 50 and 80 households in urban areas, depending on locality size, were enrolled in order to make the connection between household and locality levels possible.
- *Representativity:* the sample is representative for the Romanian household population, with a maximum sampling error of 2 percent.
- Data was not weighted.
- In-depth interviews were carried out in "face to face" sessions.

The Local Officials Survey

Sample size: 200.

Respondents: mayors, deputy mayors, local councilors, other local officials.

Sample type: theoretical.

Focus groups and semi-structured interviews: Seventeen focus groups and 33 individual in-depth interviews were carried out in six localities. The localities were selected from three counties in different provinces. Localities differed by urban/rural, level of economic development (poor versus rich communities), and ethnicity. Participating localities are as follows: Breaza, Nereju, Alunis, Focsani, Galati, Tirgu Mures.

Structure of focus groups:

- Focus groups with the poor: 6, one in each locality.
- Focus groups with Roma: 2, in Alunis and Focsani.
- Focus groups with average people: 6, one in each locality.
- Focus groups with public and private service providers, and local officials: 3, in Focsani, Galati, Tirgu Mures.
- Five in-depth individual interviews were conducted with local officials (mayors, deputy mayors, local councilors) in: Breaza, Nereju, Alunis, Focsani.
- Twenty in-depth individual interviews were conducted with public and private service providers (social workers, teachers, priests, physicians, managers of NGOs/civil organizations) distributed in all surveyed localities.
- Eight in-depth individual interviews were conducted with poor people: distributed in all surveyed localities.

REFERENCES

Anderson, M., ed. 2002. "Thinking Out Loud 3, Innovative Case Studies on Participatory Instruments." Washington, D.C.: World Bank.

Andreoni, J. 1989. "Giving with Impure Altruism: Applications to Charity and Ricardian Equivalence." *Journal of Political Economy* 97(5): 1447–1458.

Barrett, C.B. 1999. "On Pluralist Ethics and the Economics of Compassion." *Bulletin of the Association of Christian Economists* 33 (Spring): 20–35.

Barro, R.J. 1974. "Are Government Bonds Net Wealth?" *Journal of Political Economy* 82(6): 1095–1117.

Becker, G. 1974. "A Theory of Social Interactions." *Journal of Political Economy* 82(6): 1063–1093.

Boix, C. and D.N. Posner. 1998. "Social Capital: Explaining its Origins and Effects on Government Behavior." *British Journal of Political Science* 28(4):686–93.

Coate, S. 1995. "Altruism, the Samaritan's Dilemma and Government Transfer Policy." *Journal of Development Economics* 85(1): 46–57.

Coate, S. and M. Ravallion. 1993. "Reciprocity Without Commitment." *Journal of Development Economics* 40(1):1–24.

Cox, D. 2002. "Private Inter-Household Transfers in Vietnam in the Early and Late 90s." Boston College Working Papers in Economics, No. 524. Boston, MA.

Cox, D., B.E. Hansen, and E. Jimenez. 1999. "How Responsive are Private Transfers to Income? Evidence from a Laissez-Faire Economy." Boston College Working Papers in Economics, No. 329. Revised version. Boston, MA.

Cox, D., E. Jimenez, and W. Okrasa. 1996. "Family Safety Nets and Economic Transition: A study of Worker Households in Poland." Washington, D.C.: World Bank.

Cox, D. and G. Jakubson. 1995. "The Connection Between Public Transfers and Private Interfamily Transfers." *Journal of Public Economics* 57(1): 129–167.

Fukuyama, F. 1995. *Trust: Social Virtues and the Creation of Prosperity*. New York: The Free Press.

Gibson, J. G. Boe-Gibson, and F. Scrimgeour. 1998. "Are Voluntary Transfers an Effective Safety Net in Urban Papua New Guinea?" *Pacific Economic Bulletin* 13(2): 40–53.

Granovetter, M. 1974. "Getting a Job: a Study of Contacts and Careers." Cambridge, MA.: Harvard University Press.

Jimenez, E., E. Glasso, and D. Cox. 2001. "Private Transfers in Cross-Section of Developing Countries." Forthcoming in S. Knack, ed. "Social Capital and the Quality of Government: Evidence From the U.S. States." *American Journal of Political Science*, 46(4): 772–785.

King, A. and P. McDonald. 1999. "Private Transfers Across Australian Generations." NATSEM Discussion Paper, No. 41. University of Canberra, Australia.

Knack, S. 2002. "Social Capital and the Quality of Government: Evidence From the States." *American Journal of Political Science* 46(4): 772–85.

Knack, S. and P. Keefer. 1997. "Does Social Capital Have an Economic Payoff?" *Quarterly Journal of Economics* 112(4): 1251–88.

La Porta, R., F. Lopez de Silanes, A. Shleifer and R.W. Vishny. 1997. "Trust in Large Organizations." *American Economic Review Papers and Proceedings* 87(2): 333–8.

Ledeneva, A. 1998. *Russia's Economy of Favours: Blat, Networking and Informal Exchange*. Cambridge: Cambridge University Press.

Manning, N., O. Shkaratan, N Tikhonova, and K. George. 2000. *Work and Welfare in the New Russia*. Aldershot: Ashgate.

Milanovic, B. 1995. "Poverty, Inequality, and Social Policy in Transition Economies." Policy Research Working Paper, No. 1530. Washington, D.C.: The World Bank.

Morris, L. and S. Irwin. 1992. "Unemployment and informal support: dependency, exclusion or participation." *Work, Employment and Society* 6(2): 185–207.

Pahl, R.E. 1988. "Some Remarks on Informal Work, Social Polarization and the Social Structure." *International Journal of Urban and Regional Research* 12(2): 247–267.

Platteau, J. 1995. "Framework for the Analysis of Evolving Patron-Client Ties in Agrarian Economies." *World Development* 23(5): 767–786.

Putnam, R. 2000. *Bowling Alone: Collapse and Revival of American Community*. New York: Simon & Schuster.

Putnam, R. with R. Leonardi and R. Y. Nanetti. 1993. *Making Democracy Work: Civic Traditions in Modern Italy*. Princeton: Princeton University Press.

Rice, T.W. and J.L. Feldman. 1997. "Civic culture and Democracy from Europe to America." *Journal of Politics* 59(4): 1143–72.

Samuelson, P.A. 1993. "Altruism as a Problem Involving Group Versus Individual Selection in Economics and Biology." *American Economic Review* 83(2): 143–148.

Sandu, D., M.S. Stanculescu and M. Serban. 2000. "Social Assessment for Rural Development Projects: Social Needs and Actions in Romanian Villages." World Bank report. Unpublished draft.

Stanculescu, M. and I. Berevoescu. Forthcoming. "Saracie Extrema, Tranzitia Traita in Groapa de Gunoi. Romania, 2001." (Extreme Poverty, Transition Lived in a Waste Dump. Romania, 2001.) Bucharest, Romania: Research Institute for Quality of Life.

Stanculescu, M. 2002. "Romanian Households between State, Market, and Informal Economies." In R. Neef and M. Stanculescu, eds. *The Social Impact of Informal Economies in Central and Eastern Europe*. Aldershot: Ashgate.

Scott, J. 1998. *Seeing Like a State: How Certain Schemes to Improve the Human Condition Have Failed*. New Haven: Yale University Press.

Toth, J.I. and E. Sik. 2002. "Hidden Economy in Hungary 1992–1999." In R. Neef and M. Stanculescu, eds. *The Social Impact of Informal Economies in Central and Eastern Europe*. Aldershot: Ashgate.

Uslaner, E.M. 2003. "Trust and Civic Engagement in the East and the West." In G. Bodescu and E. M. Uslaner, eds. Social Capital and the Democratic Transition. New York: Routledge.

Verba, S., K.L. Schlozman, and H.E. Brady. 1995. *Voice and Equality: Civic Voluntarism in American Politics*. Cambridge, MA: Harvard University Press.

Verdery, Katherine. 1996. *What was Socialism and What Comes Next?* Princeton: Princeton University Press.

Ward-Batts, J. 2001. "Do Public Transfers Crowd Out Private Interhousehold Transfers? Responses among Lone-Mother Families in the UK." Population Studies Center Research Report, No. 01-465. University of Michigan. Ann Arbor, MI.

Wedel, J. 1986. "The Private Poland: An Anthropologist Looks at Everyday Life." New York, Facts on File.

Zak, P. and S. Knack. 2001. "Trust and Growth." *Economic Journal* 111: 295–321.

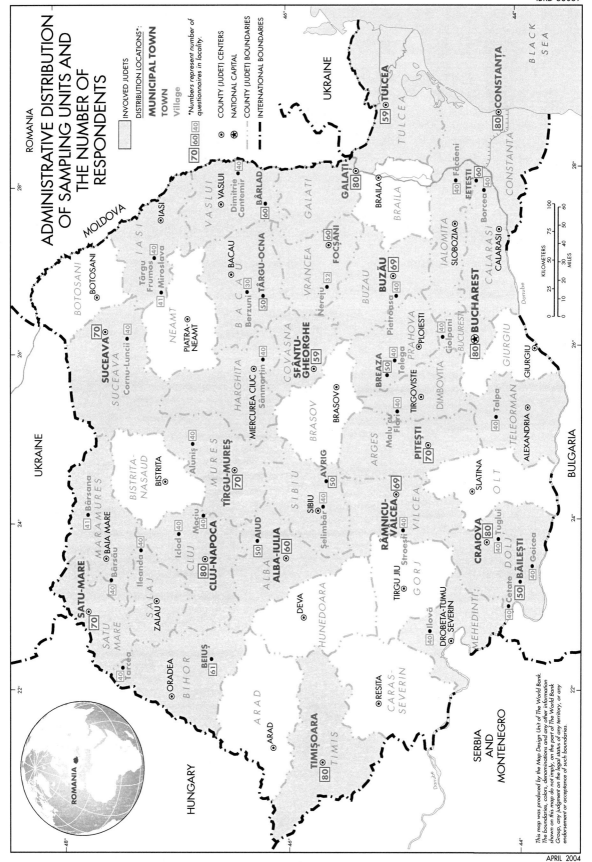

IBRD 33069

ROMANIA

ADMINISTRATIVE DISTRIBUTION
OF SAMPLING UNITS AND
THE NUMBER OF
RESPONDENTS

INVOLVED JUDETS
DISTRIBUTION LOCATIONS:
MUNICIPAL TOWN
TOWN
Village
*Numbers represent number of
questionnaires in locality.

⊙ COUNTY (JUDET) CENTERS
✹ NATIONAL CAPITAL
COUNTY (JUDET) BOUNDARIES
INTERNATIONAL BOUNDARIES

70 60 40

This map was produced by the Map Design Unit of The World Bank.
The boundaries, colors, denominations and any other information
shown on this map do not imply, on the part of The World Bank
Group, any judgment on the legal status of any territory, or any
endorsement or acceptance of such boundaries.

APRIL 2004